# Let's Go To Israel

## A Christian Guide to the Holy Land

By

Rick Hill

The author, Pastor Rick Hill, can be contacted at:

PastorRick@Rick-Hill.com
www.Rick-Hill.com

First printing, Aug. 2012
© Aug., 2012 Rick Hill
Printed in the United States. All rights reserved.

## Dedication

*This short guide to the Holy Land is dedicated to Sylvia King, whose husband, R. Edwin King (now deceased), challenged me, as a young Bible College student, to make my first trip to the Holy Land in 1969. That trip triggered in me a passion to know more about the Land, the People, and the Book that tells their story—the Bible. I hope that I can do the same.*

## Acknowledgements

This book, while my intellectual property, would never have gone to print without the help of some great people. My publisher, Mike Smitley, who has taken a risk on two of my books, Bette Runnels who offered keen, technical insights, every guest who has gone on my Holy Land tours and craved more study material, the Elders and congregation at Hillside Community Church who constantly encourage me to write more, and last, but not least, my dear Janet who puts up with my "all-nighters," my SINCERE thanks!

## Father's Press, LLC

Lee's Summit, MO
(816) 600-6288
www.fatherspress.com
e-Mail: mike@fatherspress.com

ISBN - 978-1622-872-10-7
LCCN - 2012951093

## Table of Contents

Endorsement . . . . . . . . . . . . . . . . . . . . . . . . . . . 5
About this Guide . . . . . . . . . . . . . . . . . . . . . . . . 7
Introduction . . . . . . . . . . . . . . . . . . . . . . 9

**Section I:** *Getting Ready for Your Trip*
Safety . . . . . . . . . . . . . . . . . . . . . . . . . . 13
Secure Your Home Before You Leave . . . . . . . . . . . . . . . 15
Jet Lag . . . . . . . . . . . . . . . . . . . . . . . . . . . . 17
Airplane Comfort . . . . . . . . . . . . . . . . . . . . . . . 19
Tips for Travel . . . . . . . . . . . . . . . . . . . . . . . 20
TSA Information . . . . . . . . . . . . . . . . . . . . . . . . 25
The A, B, C's of Holy Land Group Travel . . . . . . . . . . . . 26
Packing Tips . . . . . . . . . . . . . . . . . . . . . . . . . 32
Helpful Websites . . . . . . . . . . . . . . . . . . . . . . . 35
40-Days of Bible Preparation . . . . . . . . . . . . . . . . . 36
Section I Notes . . . . . . . . . . . . . . . . . . . . . . . 45

**Section II:** *Getting Acquainted with the Holy Land*
The Land . . . . . . . . . . . . . . . . . . . . . . . . . . . 49
Outline of Historical and Archaeological Periods . . . . . . . . 51
Maps . . . . . . . . . . . . . . . . . . . . . . . . . . . . . 54
Major Sites in Israel . . . . . . . . . . . . . . . . . . . . . 67
Jerusalem Supplement . . . . . . . . . . . . . . . . . . . . . 105
Israel Notes . . . . . . . . . . . . . . . . . . . . . . . . . 121
Jordan Supplement . . . . . . . . . . . . . . . . . . . . . . . 127
Major Sites in Jordan . . . . . . . . . . . . . . . . . . . . . 129

Jordan Notes . . . . . . . . . . . . . . . . . . . . . . . 136
Egypt Supplement . . . . . . . . . . . . . . . . . . . . . 141
A brief History of Egypt through the Time of Solomon . . . . . 142
Mummy Dearest . . . . . . . . . . . . . . . . . . . . . . 145
The Gods of Egypt . . . . . . . . . . . . . . . . . . . . 148
Major Sites in Egypt . . . . . . . . . . . . . . . . . . . 151
Egypt Notes . . . . . . . . . . . . . . . . . . . . . . . 157

**Section III:** *Additional Reference Material*
APPENDIX 1: Vocabulary . . . . . . . . . . . . . . . . . . 163
APPENDIX 2: Hebrew Prayers . . . . . . . . . . . . . . . . 167
APPENDIX 3: Top Archaeological Discoveries of the
                20th Century . . . . . . . . . . . . . . . . 174
APPENDIX 4: Biographical Sketches of Historical
                Figures, Groups, and Things . . . . . . . . . . 178

Additional Notes . . . . . . . . . . . . . . . . . . . . . 199

# Endorsement

*If going to Israel is like devouring a dark chocolate Oreo Cookie & Cream Klondike bar, then going to Israel with Pastor Rick Hill is like buying a 6-pack!*

*Rick loves this land and it shows. His passion for God and for God's people, Israel, oozes out of every pore as he guides you through the bustling streets of Jerusalem, hikes with you along the sandy trails of the Negev, and pauses at the pool of Bethesda to explain the history of its stirred waters and healing.*

*Beginning in 1969, when he first stepped off a tour bus onto Israeli soil, Rick's hunger to understand Israel, its people, archaeology, history, and spiritual significance has consumed him. And he didn't stop shopping for new insights and fresh applications back then, but has researched feasts of information ever since to serve up to his congregation and those fortunate enough to visit the Holy Land with him. His pet phrases, heard repeatedly as you explore a new part of the land with him, are: "This is my favorite place...until we get to the next one!" and "We're walkin'...we're walkin'!" The enthusiasm he brings to his exploration of this ancient and beloved place is infectious.*

*While his bi-annual trips to the Holy Land are high on the "bucket lists" of many people I know, not everyone will have the life changing opportunity to go to Israel with Rick in person—although you should do it if you can! Still, with this book, you can hear his love for Israel, capture his training, tap his experience, and relish the insights gained from his extensive travels throughout Israel from "Dan to Beersheba".*

*In 2012 I had the privilege to go to Israel with Rick and I can tell you from personal experience that even after 25 years of pastoring and preaching, the insights gained from that trip into the conversations Jesus had with people has come alive with new meaning. I will never again read my Bible in the same way. In preparation for the trip, and as co-host, we offered preview seminars (appetizers before the main course, if you will) to our guests. Each seminar featured a smorgasbord of tempting insights into Israel's history as well as information about what we would find when we arrived there. As a co-presenter for the meetings I prepared thoroughly to share, and yet, after each meeting I left marveling at how much Rick knew about this special place and its people.*

*I cannot endorse highly enough this new volume on exploring the land of Israel. While many traveler guides have been written on Israel, I know of no other book that does it so well, with such attention to detail, or with such a passion for its people. I predict that this book will become a classic for anyone planning his or her once-in-a-lifetime trip to Israel.*

Dr. Douglas Baker<br>
Senior Pastor, Faith Community Church by the Sea<br>
Professor, BIOLA College

## About this Guide

This guide is useful whether you are traveling to Israel with a group or studying about Israel in your home. It is filled with practical information that will enhance your tour experience and deepen your personal knowledge of the land of the Bible and Bible times.

It is designed to help both young and mature Christ-followers to grow in their knowledge of the Scriptures. But it can be used by anyone interested in knowing more about Israel, Christ-follower or not.

There are a variety of maps, and personal photos in this guide. I created most of them with Accordance Software and Pages Software, which will be consistent throughout the guide. I have noted the ones I did not make. The maps and photos will help you to visualize the topic or land area you are reading about.

There is a list of the major sites in Israel, Jordan, and Egypt in alphabetical order, along with many biblical references to assist you in finding out more about the various sites in the Holy Land.

Many people who travel to Israel wonder about communicating with the locals on their trip. This is a problem that you will hardly ever experience on a tour. However, to get a feel for the language, there is a section of important words and phrases that will be helpful on your trip.

There are biographies of many important historical and biblical characters. Learning about them in advance will enhance your time in Israel. They will come alive as you see them in the context of their time.

Finally, to organize the material, I have divided this guide into three sections:

- Section I: *Getting Ready for the Trip*
- Section II: *Getting Acquainted with the Holy Land*
- Section III: *Additional Reference Material*

I have told the many guests on my tours that with just a ten-day trip to the Holy Land, they will know as much or more Bible history and geography than most first year Bible College students. I believe this to be true. When you can put the events, places, and characters of the Bible in their context, it really comes alive. You will never read your Bible the same again!

Happy traveling, everyone!

# Introduction

Have you, like me, ever wondered what really took place with a biblical character at a specific location when you read about it in the Bible? I have. Many times! I have conjured up all kinds of images and thought I had a fairly good grasp of the subject. Then I made my first trip to Israel in 1969, over forty years ago as of this writing. I must tell you, I was in for the shock of my life.

Let's just take the story of Moses on Mt. Nebo for example. He was not allowed into the "land flowing with milk and honey" because he had disobeyed God by striking a rock for water instead of speaking to it. (See Numbers 20:1-12 and Deuteronomy 34:1-6)

In my mind, I had Moses on a mountaintop like Everest and as he stood there, he closed his eyes and had a vision of the land. In my mind, I saw him as a cartoon character with an idea bubble above his head. "This is what the Land looks like," God said to him, in my mind.

Well, that image crashed and burned on my first visit to Mt. Nebo. I've stood there. It's only about 3,000 ft above sea level—no Mt. Everest at all. Even with my poor eyesight and on a smoggy day (I don't think there was smog to interfere with Moses' view), I could easily see the Dead Sea, Jericho, and the lush Jordan Valley. Interestingly, other major cities weren't that far away: Bethlehem (30 miles), Jerusalem (25 miles). Even the Sea of Galilee didn't seem far from there to me (about 75 miles).

When God said He showed the Land to Moses, Moses saw the Land. That is just one of many crash and burn sessions I have had on my visits to the Holy Land. So now, what was once obscure has been cleared up. I read the account in the Bible, but I read it with a different geographical lens, and it makes perfect sense.

Other phrases I read in Scripture make more sense now. A simple phrase like *"they went up to Jerusalem,"* leaps off the page because I have gone "up" to Jerusalem.

As you read this short work in preparation for your trip to the Holy Land, you are about to embark on a truly life-changing experience. The Israeli Department of Tourism makes the claim: "Visit Israel — Your life will never be the same!" I wholeheartedly agree. Your trip will have a profound impact on you and your Christian experience going forward.

As you are preparing for your trip, don't hesitate to read and re-read Section I: *Getting Ready for the Trip*. In it I make suggestions and offer a lot of information to help in your preparation for the trip; tips that will even make your packing easier!

When you sign up for your tour and/or receive the itinerary, begin looking up the sites. Learn about them. In Section II: *Getting to Know the Holy Land,* I have listed over 80 major sites by country in alphabetical order in this guide. If you are computer savvy, look up the places on the Internet. It is a valuable resource of information. You can also get more information and photos about the Holy Land from my blogs, Holy Land Pics and Holy Land Places at www.Rick-Hill.com

I also suggest that you take this guide with you on your tour. It can serve as supplement information to that which you receive from your guide. Earmark pages daily so that you can use bus time to read up on the next stop. You want to get as much information as you can from your tour. This book will help you both before you go, and while you are there.

When God finally permitted the Children of Israel to go into the Land, Moses sent out spies to investigate it. The words He spoke to them are words that you can take to heart for your trip. "*...See what the land is like: whether the people who dwell in it are strong or weak, few or many; whether the land they dwell in is good or bad; whether the cities they inhabit are like camps or strongholds; whether the land* *is rich or poor; and whether there are forests there or not..."* (Numbers 13:18-20a NKJV)

Later at Mt. Horeb, God sent them away from the mountain saying, *"You have stayed at this mountain long enough. It is time to break camp and move on. Go to the hill country of the Amorites and to all the neighboring regions—the Jordan Valley, the hill country, the western foothills, the Negev, and the coastal plain. Go to the land of the Canaanites and to Lebanon, and all the way to the great Euphrates River. I am giving all this land to you!"* (Deuteronomy 1:6-8a NLT)

You will do that on your trip. You will see the hill country, the western foothills, the Negev, the Jordan Valley, and the coastal plain. You will witness for yourself whether the people are strong or weak, few or many, if the Land is good or bad, rich or poor, or even if there are forests there or not.

Traveling to the Holy Land has had a profound impact on my life. I hope and pray it does the same for you!

Rick Hill
Julian, California

# Section I: *Getting Ready for Your Trip*

**Safety**

Without a doubt, the number one question I get from people at orientation meetings when considering a trip to the Holy Land is: Is it safe?

I wish I could dispel all your doubts and fears in this book, but I really don't know how to do that. I can only tell you that in all my trips there, I have never had any fear of safety.

Maybe this will help you. Upon returning from my trips, I have a reunion to celebrate the trip and to renew acquaintances. The first question I ask of them is: Did you feel safe? I have yet to have anyone answer in the negative. Not one!

Another thing that has helped me to get the bigger picture was a conversation I had with a tour company owner many years ago. He told me in the thirty-plus years he had been organizing tours, not even a single guest had been evacuated for safety concerns. He told me about evacuations for medical emergencies, family and business issues, and things of that nature—but none for safety!

Finally, I have found that for many, their perception of the danger in going to the Holy Land has a lot to do with the media and how they represent events there. At one of our reunions a man admitted, "I thought I would see a terrorist behind every bush." Nothing could be farther from the truth. You are more likely to be injured driving from your home to the airport for your trip than of being attacked by a terrorist on your tour.

That being said, there are some things that you can do to avoid exposure to uncomfortable incidents:

- Always stay with your group and don't wander off to explore things on your own. Your guide and driver, by keeping in touch with tour operators, are knowledgeable of potentially troublesome areas and will avoid those places.

- Remain low-keyed in your behavior and dress. Loud and obnoxious behavior only draws attention in your direction. Likewise, avoid wearing clothing that announces your nationality or advertises your side of a political conflict. On my first trip to the Holy Land, my tour host and mentor said, "Avoid the 'Ugly American' stereotype." Those words are just as valuable today.

## Secure Your Home Before You Leave

Your time away from home will be more peaceful if you have taken precautions to protect it while you are on your tour. Here are a few tips to consider:

- Install secure locks on all doors and windows.

- Never leave your house key hidden outside your home while you are away.

- Store your valuables in a safe-deposit box.

- Turn the ringer on your telephone down so that no one is alerted to your absence by the constant unanswered ringing.

- Don't announce your absence on the message of your answering machine or on any social media like FaceBook, Twitter, Match.com, etc.

- Ask a trusted neighbor to watch the house while you're away. Leave your travel schedule and contact information with them so that you can be reached in the event of an emergency.

- Stop all deliveries or arrange for a neighbor to pick up your mail, newspapers, and packages.

- Have a neighbor place garbage cans at the curb on your normal pickup days, and return them to their proper place after the garbage has been picked up.

- Arrange for someone to mow and maintain your yard to give your home that lived-in look.

- Plug in and activate timers to turn on your lights, TV, and Radio at appropriate times.

- Leave your blinds, shades, and curtains in their normal position.

- Ask a neighbor to occasionally park on your driveway. If you leave your car at home, park it as you normally would. Have a neighbor move it from time to time to appear that it is being used.

- Secure storage sheds, attic entrances, and gates.

- Check with your local Sheriff's Department. Many of them will do a "vacation drive-by" if notified.

## Jet Lag

Traveling to Israel, or any foreign country for that matter, can be fun, interesting, and exciting, but because of the distance, one must deal with the consequences of long flights. Going from time zone to time zone can produce what is commonly known as jet lag. Jet lag occurs when your body says, "Stay awake," when it is the middle of the night at your destination. The opposite is also true. Your body may yell at you to, "Go to bed, you're sleepy," when it is actually the middle of the afternoon.

There was a time when jet lag was considered to be a state of mind, but now we know it is the result of your biological clock being out of sync with your new time zone. Your biological clock, medically speaking, is the rhythm of the rise and fall of your body's temperature and hormones, and other biological conditions.

There are no sure fire tricks to avoid jet lag, but forethought and good planning may help diminish its effects. Even small adjustments in behavior before, during, and after the arrival at your destination may help shorten its hold on you.

I have now traveled to over 50 countries and have firsthand experience when it comes to jet lag. Here are some things I've learned from my personal physician, travel magazines, and the Internet that have helped me to overcome the effects of jet lag.

- When you board the plane, set your watch to the time zone of your destination and try to follow a sleep pattern in it.

- Avoid alcohol and caffeine a minimum of 3 hours before sleeping. Both of these act as stimulants and prevent sleep.

- When trying to sleep on airplanes, use blindfolds and earplugs to block out light and dampen noise levels.

- When you arrive at your destination, avoid heavy meals.

- When you have arrived at your destination, stay up until 10:00 PM local time. If for some reason you must sleep during the day, take a short nap. Be sure to set an alarm and sleep no longer than a half an hour.

- Get as much sunlight as you can upon arrival at your destination. Daylight is a powerful tool to regulate your biological clock.

- Avoid heavy exercise close to your new bedtime.

Regardless of what you've heard, the types of food you eat will most likely have little or no effect on minimizing jet lag.

There are many things that affect your sleep: noise, sleep surface, heat/cold, and altitude just to name a few. Your age and gender may also play a role in sleeping patterns. You can assist in modifying your behavior with approved, prescription sleep aids. Always consult your physician for products that are safe and effective. One over-the-counter product that is effective for some people is Melatonin. There is evidence that melatonin increases the tendency to sleep, but it does not affect the amount of sleep at night. Still, you should consult with your physician before using it.

**Airplane Comfort**

Flying for long periods of time in a dry, cramped plane can be, as my physician once told me, "The perfect incubator for germs." You want to arrive at your destination feeling healthy and refreshed, but how do you do that? Here are a few tips:

- Drink plenty of water before, during, and after your flight. Don't refuse any offer of water from your cabin steward.

- Take healthy snacks with you on the trip. Health bars, nuts, and dried fruit are good ideas. Make sure you don't take any restricted items that will be confiscated at your destination (fresh fruit, particularly).

- Get up regularly and stretch your limbs.

- Do seat exercises regularly to keep your circulation moving. Airplane Yoga may be just the thing for you. For more details see: http://www.cnngo.com

- Wear comfortable, loose fitting clothing as much as possible.

- Pack a spare pair of underwear and or a shirt/blouse to change into before landing. Never underestimate the power of clean clothes to help you feel fresh at the end of a long flight.

## Tips for Travel

American Embassy in Israel

> 71 Hayarkon Street, Tel Aviv
> The American Consulate in Jerusalem
> 18 Agron Road, Jerusalem
>
> Both offices are open 8:00-11:00 AM, Monday - Friday.

Business Hours

Most stores open/close with appropriate hours to accommodate their customers. It is not uncommon for a store to close in the middle of the day for an hour or two. Jewish shops will also close on the Shabbat, Friday evening at sunset, and will not reopen until Saturday evening at sunset.

Climate

The weather pattern in Israel is similar to that of Los Angeles County, USA. Winters are short, but at times can be very cold. Rainfall is mostly limited from November to April. The warmest places in Israel lie in areas below sea level.

Currency

The currency of Israel is called the new shekel (NIS), which is divided into 100 agorot. You can exchange money at the airport, banks and in hotels. Most all of the places visited on a Holy Land tour will accept USD. ATM and major credit cards are also accepted.

Jordan's currency is the Jordanian Dinar (JD), which is divided into 100 Piastres.

Egypt's currency is the Egyptian Pound (E£), which is divided into

100 Piastres.

## Customs Regulations

As a general rule, returning U.S. residents are allowed to bring $800.00 worth of merchandise purchased abroad duty-free. For detailed regulations, check out the U.S. Customs website:
www. customs.treas.gov

- You must be abroad 48 hours.

- Merchandise totaling $800.00 must be based on fair retail value of the country from which they are purchased.

- Gifts may be mailed or shipped to the U.S. duty-free, but make sure you are aware of the restrictions. For details, contact the U.S. Customs authority.

## Documentation

A valid Passport is the only official document you will need to travel throughout the Holy Land, but it is recommended that you take along another form of ID as well. Guard your passport and keep it secured at all times.

## Electricity

Israel works on a current of 220/240 volts. Almost all newer U.S. electronics have built-in converters and run on both 110/240v. All that is necessary for most appliances is an adaptor. Although Israel has three-pronged outlets, a two-prong adapter is best because it will also fit in Jordanian sockets as well.

Your electronic device will tell you if

it runs on both currents, but you may need good eyes to see it. Just look something like: 100v-240v, 50/60Hz.

Here is an example of my battery charger.

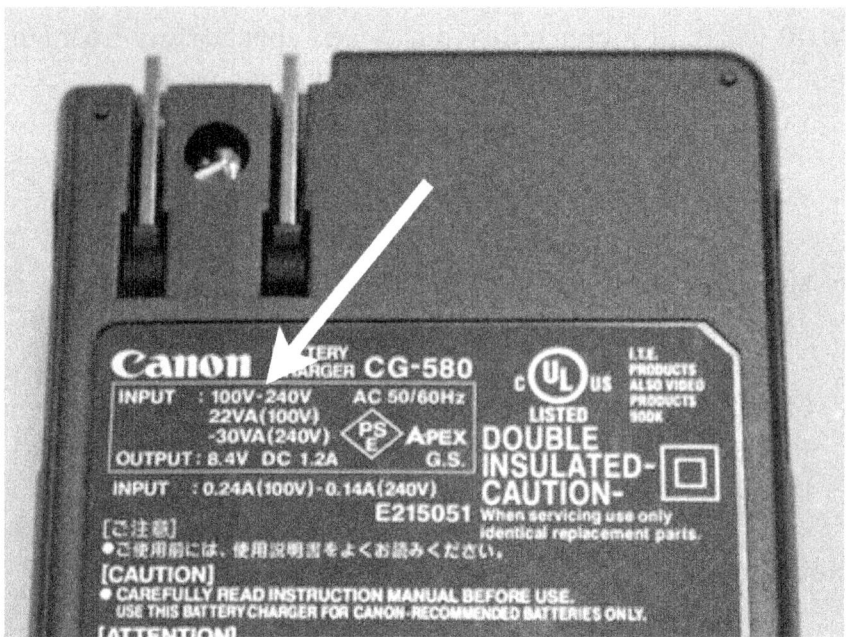

Geography

Israel is a small country about the size of New Jersey whose entire west coast is exposed to the Mediterranean Sea. It is bordered by Lebanon to the north, Syria to the northeast, Jordan to the east and south, and Egypt to the southwest. From north to south, Israel is less than 300 miles in length. At its widest point, it is about 70 miles. Despite its small size, Israel has a diverse terrain. (See a topographical map of Israel on page 50)

Government

Israel is a parliamentary democracy. A President—Chief of State—is elected by the Knesset (Parliament) for a five-year term. The head of the government is the Prime Minister. He/she is elected by popular vote and may serve a four-year term. The legislative body is the Knesset (120 members), elected by popular vote for a four-year term.

Holidays and Festivals

More than likely, you will not be on a tour during a National festival or holiday. It is very likely, though, that you will be there on a Shabbat. The Shabbat begins Friday evening at sunset and ends on Saturday evening at sunset. Virtually all Jewish businesses, government offices, and transportation shut down. (Hotels and other businesses that cater to tourists may have staff available for service).

The major Jewish holidays are:

- Rosh Ha-Shanah - New Years (September)

- Yom Kippur - Day of Atonement and ending of the New Year celebration. (September/October)

- Sukkot and Simchas Torrah - the Feast of Tabernacles and the Rejoicing in the Law, is an annual pilgrim festival. (September/October)

- Purim - The story of Esther. It has an almost carnival like atmosphere. (February/March)

- Pesach - An annual pilgrim festival, Passover celebrates the Exodus from Egypt. (March/April)

- Shavuot: An annual pilgrim festival, the Feast of Pentecost commemorates the harvest (May/June).

- Hanukkah: The Festival of Lights (December)

Religions

Jewish 80%
Muslim 15% (mostly Sunni)
Christian 2%
Other 3%

Shopping—Things that you might consider purchasing in Israel:

- Diamonds
- Jewelry
- Woodwork (especially olive wood)
- Leather goods (including fashion items)
- Copper and Brass
- Artwork

Shopping in the Middle East can be an exciting experience because you can barter for everything (unless the shop has a 'fixed price' sign posted). Don't settle for the asking price of any item. If you are not comfortable with the price, just walk away. My Father was fond of saying, "If you paid more than you wanted to, and the guy got less than he wanted, you've probably settled on a good price."

Travel Insurance

Travel insurance is highly recommended. You can choose from a simple trip cancellation policy to a comprehensive policy that includes: health, luggage, and trip cancellation. Your own insurance company may carry trip insurance or they may have a good recommendation. Two companies (as of the current printing) that come highly recommended are:

http://www.travelguard.com  and  http://www.aaintl.com

# TSA Information

The following is the latest information from the TSA website regarding liquids with your carry-on luggage:

3-1-1 for carry-on = 3 ounce bottle or less; 1 quart-sized, clear, plastic, zip-top bag; 1 bag per passenger placed in screening bin. One-quart bag per person limits the total liquid volume each traveler can bring. 3 oz container size is a security measure.

Be prepared! Each time TSA searches a carry-on it slows down the line. Practicing 3-1-1 will ensure a faster and easier checkpoint experience.

3-1-1 is for short trips. If in doubt, put your liquids in checked luggage.

Declare larger liquids. Prescription medications, baby formula and milk (when traveling with an infant or toddler) are allowed in reasonable quantities exceeding three ounces and are not required to be in the zip-top bag. Declare these items for inspection at the checkpoint.

For the most current TSA information go to:

http://www.tsa.gov/311

# The A, B, C's of Holy Land Group Travel

Adapter - Bring a plug adapter for anything that needs electricity or recharging. You will not need a transformer if your appliance reads 50-60 Hz and 110-240V. (See pages 21-22)

Be - on time, flexible, and have a good sense of humor! Every day is a learning, exploring and worshipping experience. Your attitude may affect the morale of the entire tour—for better or worse.

Clothes - Bring comfortable clothing and don't waste your efforts packing formal wear. Israel is very informal. Ladies may wish to wear slacks on the trip. Men should wear the same. Remember when packing, think layers, and less is better. Wash and wear items are very helpful. Shorts are acceptable but if you wear them you should also bring a "modesty kit" on the bus for those times when you visit churches and shrines. A "modesty kit" for men and women means, knees and shoulders covered—and men, covering for the head. Ball caps and hats are considered covering. Paper yarmulkes are usually provided at the Western Wall Plaza (Kotel) where covering is necessary.

Dining - Buffet breakfast and dinners are served daily on most group tours. It is <u>not</u> a good idea to skip breakfast. Israeli hotels serve a bountiful and nutritious breakfast with a variety of entrées. The evening meals are also plentiful with ample selections. On a group tour, lunch stops are typically at a variety of local cuisines with food types that are somewhat familiar. Likewise, the places will be safe and clean.

Exercise - Israel is a land of rocky hills, valleys, and rough terrain. It may seem that you will be walking uphill more than downhill. I recommended that you begin a daily walking regimen to condition yourself. A mile each day is a good, healthy start.

Footwear - The terrain is mostly rocky or hard and uneven. Bring sturdy but comfortable walking shoes. Non-skid soles are also important during the wet season. There will be numerous walks and possible hikes along nature trails with occasional rugged places. A pair of water shoes is advisable for the swimming sites, especially the Dead Sea as it is very rocky along the shoreline.

Get - everything you need for the trip before you leave the U.S. You'll find the price on common things you purchase here much more expensive when traveling internationally.

Health - No shots or vaccinations are needed to visit Israel at this time. If you need medication, be sure to carry it with you. It is a good idea to travel with certain items such as, Pepto Bismol, Imodium, sleeping aids or Dramamine to overcome jet lag and/or motion sickness. Pharmacies may not always be convenient to the schedule, so it's a good idea to pack aspirin, Band-Aids and other small essentials. Short-term health insurance policies for travelers are a must when going abroad. This type of policy is easily obtainable from most insurance companies. If you feel a health issue coming on—major or minor—do not hesitate to call a physician. Nearly all hotels have doctors available on call. Most travel insurance will cover these costs (some by reimbursement) so read your policy carefully.

Identification - Bring other identification with you in addition to your passport. ALWAYS keep your passport in your possession. Make copies of all your identification and credit cards in the event yours are lost or stolen. Keep your document copies in a safe place.

Just in case - you want to connect with your loved ones or friends, the Internet is best. Most of the hotels will have wireless connection (mostly free, but some at a cost). If you haven't done so already, download and learn to use SKYPE or iCHAT (for Mac). With either of these programs you can use the Internet to see and talk with your loved ones and friends FREE! If you prefer phones, check with your provider to see if they offer international plans.

Know the weather pattern - With the modern convenience of computers and smart phones, it's much easier to know the forecast for weather patterns up to seven days in advance. This will help you from over or under packing for your trip. Bookmark your favorite weather website and check it regularly.

Luggage - You are permitted <u>ONE</u> suitcase and <u>ONE</u> carry-on bag (excluding purse or camera/computer bag) per person. Be sure your suitcase closes and fastens securely (use extra straps if necessary). The dimensions should not exceed 62 inches in length and width and depth, and not over 50 lbs in weight. Mark your suitcase and/or carry-on bag clearly so you will be able to easily distinguish it.

Concerning liquids, see the current TSA 3-1-1 policy in this guide (page 25). In addition to the carry on luggage, the following items may be carried on board: a handbag, camera case, or computer case (these must fit under your seat), an umbrella or walking stick (or other orthopedic aide), and reading material. NEVER attempt to board a plane with weapons of any kind, fake weapons, pointed or sharp objects (e.g. scissors, knives, knitting needles, fingernail clippers, etc.), or any other dangerous item.

Money - Plan to spend approximately $250 for incidental food items (beverages, snacks, lunch, etc.). You will also want to bring money to purchase souvenirs. You will be wise to carry $50 in one dollar bills with the rest in $5, $10, and $20 denominations. You can exchange dollars into local currency at airports, hotels, and banks abroad. Most stores love U.S. dollars but you will get all your change in that country's currency. ATM machines are available in many locations. Larger purchases can be made using a major credit card. I suggest taking only one credit card with you on the trip. Make sure your bank and/or Credit Card Company is aware that you will be using your card outside the U.S. on very specific dates.

Not covered - in the price of your tour are items such as phone calls, room service, bar privileges, excess luggage charges, credit card fees, souvenirs, medical expenses, and other incidental extras. Be sure to check your group package price. Some package deals do not include gratuities, airport fees and taxes, entry fees (visas and border crossing), and other common expenses. These charges can really add up, so make sure you know what you are getting in your group deal.

Other essential items - a Bible and notebook/diary. You might consider a mini recorder if you'd like to record the orientation and Bible studies. (See pages 32-34) for essential items to consider taking on your tour)

Passport - Each person will need a valid passport that will not expire less than 6 months beyond the touring dates (specifically 6 months beyond the return date). Airlines will not allow anyone to board a plane to Israel without fulfilling this important precondition. If you don't have a passport or need to renew your passport, be sure to allow enough time for processing. Your tour host will need your passport number, country of origin, and expiration date to secure your tourist visas and airline tickets. NEVER, I repeat, NEVER leave your passport in your hotel room.

Queasiness - You will be traveling by air and land. The degree of motion sickness can range from mild discomfort to severe incapacitation. Symptoms are usually short-lived, resolving themselves with the cessation of movement. If you are prone to motion sickness consult your physician for prescribed medication.

Read - all the custom regulation material you receive, keep them handy, and properly report your purchases as directed. Keeping a record of your purchases will make the filing of your customs report easier.

Seating arrangements - (Airlines) The final authority for seating preferences rests with the cooperation of the airlines. Check with your agent should you have medical requirements for special seating. Likewise, your agent can help you if you are interested in upgrading your seats. You should make these arrangements as early as possible. (Tour Bus) Regarding bus seats for your daily sightseeing, it's best to extend courtesy to other passengers by rotating your seats so that everyone is insured a seat up front with the guide.

Treat - your host country with respect. An old proverb says, "He who treats his host with respect shall in turn be treated as an honored guest." Leave only footprints and take only photographs. Do not take away "souvenirs" from historical sites and natural areas.

Utilize - every means to educate yourself about the geography, customs, manners, and culture of the regions you plan to visit.

Value Added Tax - Most shops in Israel have already included the tax in the price you pay for your goods—as of this writing, 16%. There are a few stores that offer a rebate of your tax when you purchase $100 or more. The stores that offer the rebate have the information prominently displayed. You will receive the rebate form, your receipt, and the procedure to get your rebate at the airport upon your departure.

Witnessing - Let your life and conduct count! Consider the missionaries and believers there, whose lot we might make more difficult by arousing anger or by giving a poor testimony.

eXemptions - Don't buy any products made from endangered plants or animals, such as ivory, tortoise shell, animal skins and feathers. Read "Know Before You Go," the U.S. Customs list of products that cannot be imported.

www.cbp.gov/xp/cgov/travel/vacation/kbyg/

You - will get brochures at many of the sites you visit. Keep them at least until you return home. They may be valuable in helping you to sort through your photos or to remember some important information that you would otherwise have forgotten.

Z - any last questions? Let's get ready to travel!

## Packing Tips

Here are some suggestions for packing for your trip of a lifetime.

MOST IMPORTANT...take only one suitcase. If you have no space left in your suitcase, you are taking too much. Unpack and start again! A general rule of thumb for packing is this: 25% of the clothes and other objects that most travelers take will NOT be utilized on a tour.

And this is the best advice I've ever received for a group tour to the Holy Land. Start a "travel drawer/box" at your home and put into it all your socks, underwear, and shirts that are just beginning to get holes in them, or that have worn out elastic, or that you never intend to wear again. Pack them for your trip. Then after you wear them, discard them. That way, your suitcase will begin to empty out and you'll have room for all the souvenirs you plan to buy.

The following are suggested items only. You may want to customize the list for your personal needs.

- Medical (ALWAYS consult your physician)

    a small, medical First-Aid travel kit
    all prescription drugs
    copies of prescriptions (in case they need refilling)
    antacid tablets
    acetaminophen (fever)
    ibuprofen (muscle pain)
    motion sickness pills
    sleeping pills
    antiseptic spray
    nasal spray
    cough lozenges
    hydrocortisone cream (skin irritation)
    anti-fungal cream (athletes' foot)
    antibiotic ointment (skin infections)

fiber tablets (constipation)
loperamide tablets (diarrhea)
sterile syringes and needles (if necessary)
hot and cold packs
insect repellent
eye drops/contact lens solution
sunscreen/sunburn medication/ointment-lotion

- Toiletries (Hotels will provide soap, body wash, lotion, and shampoo)

    personal hygiene products
    toothbrush/paste
    mouthwash/floss
    deodorant
    tissue/handkerchief
    towelettes
    Q-Tips
    lens wipes
    makeup
    comb/brush
    shaving needs

- Wardrobe (modest with no advertising)

    under garments and socks
    shorts/slacks/jeans
    shirts/blouses
    jacket/sweater/scarf
    swimsuit/beach apparel
    good walking shoes!
    aqua socks/flip-flops (especially good at the Dead Sea)
    sunglasses/umbrella
    hat (wide-brim is best)

- Miscellaneous

    tote bag/backpack for day trips
    plastic bags (for laundry, wet beach items, etc.)
    travel alarm
    travel sewing kit
    binoculars
    pen/notebook-diary/Bible
    extra film or memory devices (digital equipment)
    small recording device
    batteries
    EXTRA pair of prescription glasses/sunglasses

- For the plane

    airline tickets
    valid passport
    emergency change of clothing
    essential toiletries (See TSA rules for liquids page 25)
    books or digital reader/iPod/iPad type devices
    blindfold/ear plugs
    neck pillow

## Helpful Websites

About passport information:
    http://www.travel.state.gov/passport

About health/insurance:
    http://www.cdc.gov/travel
    http://www.travelguard.com
    http://www. aaintl.com

About currency conversion:
    http://www.oanda.com/convert/classic

About travel:
    http://www.travel.state.gov/travel
    http://www.gbp.gov (customs)
    http://www.tsa.gov/311
    http://www.goisrael.com
    http://www.visitjordan.com
    http://www.gotoegypt.org
    http://www.weather.com

About current affairs:
    http://www.jpost.com (Jerusalem Post)

About Judaism and Islam:
    http://www.religionfacts.com (a good primer on Judaism)
    http://www.mfa.gov.il/MFA/facts

About the Holy Land:
    http://www.bibleplaces.com
    http://www.jewishvirtuallibrary.org
    http://www.bib-arch.org
    http://www.rehov.org

About the Temple:
    http://www.templemount.org

## 40-Days of Bible Preparation

Now that you have a plan to physically prepare for your trip, don't forget to prepare for your trip spiritually. First and foremost, you can begin praying about it. Thank the Lord for the opportunity to go. Pray for a safe trip. Pray for those who lead the trip: your tour company, host, guide, driver, hotel operators, food handlers, fellow travelers, etc.

Below you will find a great way to time your departure with a daily schedule of Bible reading and prayer. This is a 40-day devotion to prepare you for your Holy Land experience. When you know the date of your departure, plan this daily devotional to end the day before your trip.

Day 40
Scripture: Acts 9:32-41
Place: Joppa, Lydda (p. 65)
Event: Healing of Aeneas and Dorcas
Meditation: God heals; in this life or the next. Take time to thank Him for that.

Day 39
Scripture: Acts 9:42-10:48
Place: Caesarea (p. 65)
Event: Peter received a vision
Meditation: God is no respecter of persons. Thank Him for that.

Day 38
Scripture: Song of Solomon 2:1
Place: Plain of Sharon (p. 50)
Event: The Rose of Sharon
Meditation: Few gifts in life are more wonderful than a spouse or friend who radiates the Lord. Thank Him for that.

Day 37
Scripture: Ezekiel 34:11-16
Place: The Mediterranean (p. 50)
Event: The re-gathering of the Jewish people
Meditation: God fulfills His promises. Take time to thank Him for that.

Day 36
Scripture: 1st Kings 18
Place: Mt. Carmel (p. 66)
Event: Elijah vs the Prophets of Ba-al
Meditation: God vindicates His truth, His reputation, and His faithful servant. Praise Him with that in mind.

Day 35
Scripture: Luke 1:26-80
Place: Nazareth (p. 61)
Event: The childhood home of Jesus
Meditation: God puts us in a place where we can be most used by Him. Be submissive and thank Him with that in mind.

Day 34
Scripture: John 2:1-12
Place: Cana (p. 61)
Event: Jesus' first miracle (turning water into wine)
Meditation: In Jesus, God has given us the best and will continue to do so. Praise Him with that in mind.

Day 33
Scripture: Matthew 4:12-17
Place: Sea of Galilee (p. 60)
Event: Jesus moved His ministry headquarters to Capernaum
Meditation: God has revealed Himself so that we can live in light, not darkness. Thank Him with that in mind.

Day 32
Scripture: Luke 8:22-25
Place: Sea of Galilee (p. 60)
Event: Jesus calmed the storm
Meditation: God is sovereign over all things. What do I have to fear? Worship Him in light of that.

Day 31
Scripture: Matthew 5:1-6, 28
Place: Mt. of Beatitudes (p. 66)
Event: Sermon on the Mount
Meditation: God's principles for kingdom living are always best to follow. Praise Him in light of that.

Day 30
Scripture: Matthew 14:13-21
Place: Tabgha (p. 102)
Event: Feeding the multitudes
Meditation: God has resources to take care of us in the most sufficient and ample way. Worship Him for that.

Day 29
Scripture: John 21:1-14
Place: Sea of Galilee (p. 60)
Event: Jesus appeared to His disciples
Meditation: God desires us to have fellowship with Him through His Son. Even betrayal on our part does not stop His pursuit. Praise Him for that.

Day 28
Scripture: Luke 7:1-10
Place: Capernaum (p. 60 insert)
Event: Healing of the Centurion's Son
Meditation: God honors faith because faith honors Him. Pray to Him in light of that.

Day 27
Scripture: Matthew 8:28-34
Place: Kursi (p. 60 insert)
Event: Jesus delivered the demoniac
Meditation: Greater is He who is in us than he who is in the world. Thank Him with that in mind.

Day 26
Scripture: Matthew 14:22-33
Place: Sea of Galilee (p. 60)
Event: Jesus walked on water
Meditation: God is with us in the storms of life. Thank Him for that.

Day 25
Scripture: Matthew 16:13-20
Place: Caesarea Philippi (Banias) (p. 60)
Event: Peter confessed Jesus as the Christ
Meditation: God will build His church; the church will uphold His name. Praise Him in light of that.

Day 24
Scripture: Matthew 17:1-13
Place: Mt. Hermon (p. 66)
Event: The transfiguration of Jesus
Meditation: His name is worthy to be upheld. There is none like Him; past, present, or future. Honor Him in light of that.

Day 23
Scripture: 1st Kings 12:25-33
Place: Dan (p. 60)
Event: Jeroboam built a horned altar
Meditation: God is jealous for His own name. Worship Him with that in mind.

Day 22
Scripture: Joshua 11:1-20

(day 22 cont.)
Place: Hazor (p. 60)
Event: The Israelite conquest
Meditation: God's judgment seems late at times, but He does not forget. Praise Him for that.

Day 21
Scripture: Judges 4:1-5, 31
Place: Mt. Tabor (p. 66)
Event: Deborah defeated Sisera
Meditation: True victory is not experienced until we return praise to Him. Offer your praise to God.

Day 20
Scripture: Judges 7:1-25
Place: En Harod (Gideon Spring) (p. 61)
Event: Gideon fought the Midianites
Meditation: God chooses to act the most decisively when the odds seem their worst. Praise Him with that in mind.

Day 19
Scripture: 1st Samuel 31:1-13
Place: Beth Shean (p. 61)
Event: Saul terminated his life
Meditation: It's not how well you start, but how well you finish. Pray with that in mind.

Day 18
Scripture: Joshua 6:1-27
Place: Jericho (p. 63)
Event: Joshua and the wall of Jericho
Meditation: When life is uncertain, take a risk or else you will gain nothing. Pray with that in mind.

Day 17
Scripture: Matthew 4:1-11

(day 17 cont.)
Place: Mt. of Temptation (on the outskirt of Jericho, p. 63)
Event: Jesus was tempted by Satan
Meditation: The strongest resistance against temptation is knowing who you are and never doubting God's Word. Pray with that in mind.

Day 16
Scripture: Ezekiel 47:1-13
Place: The Dead Sea (p. 63)
Event: The Dead Sea will become fresh
Meditation: By God's grace, our deadness is made new. Praise Him for that.

Day 15
Scripture: 1st Samuel 24
Place: En Gedi (p. 63)
Event: David met Saul
Meditation: Wise people let God act for them. Pray with that in mind.

Day 14
Scripture: Psalm 57
Place: En Gedi (p. 63)
Event: David fled from Saul
Meditation: We have confidence that God is faithful. Praise Him with that in mind.

Day 13
Scripture: Psalm 63
Place: the Judean Wilderness (p. 50)
Event: David writes Psalms to the Lord
Meditation: God satisfies our lives in both prosperous times and lean times. Thank Him for that.

Day 12
Scripture: Luke 10:25-37
Place: Road to Jericho

(day 12 cont.)
Event: The Good Samaritan
Meditation: Living like Jesus means changing the question from, who is my neighbor, to how can I help my neighbor. Pray with that in mind.

Day 11
Scripture: Psalm 120-134
Place: Temple Mount (see Mt. Moriah, p. 66)
Event: Recited as Jews go to the Temple for worship
Meditation: True worship comes from a clean and undivided heart determined to live life for the common good. Worship Him in light of that.

Day 10
Scripture: Genesis 22
Place: Mt. Moriah (Jerusalem) (p. 66)
Event: Abraham was obedient to God's command
Meditation: The one who loves God will obediently surrender to Him, trusting in His provision. Thank Him for His provision.

Day 9
Scripture: 1st Chronicles 11:4-8
Place: The City of David (see Jerusalem, p. 63)
Event: David defeated the Jebusites
Meditation: If a man's ways are pleasing to the Lord, He will make even his enemies to bow down. Thank Him for that.

Day 8
Scripture: Matthew 1:18-2:12
Place: Bethlehem (p. 63)
Event: The Birth of Jesus
Meditation: Jesus became one of us so that it could be said God is for us, and God is with us. Praise Him for that.

Day 7
Scripture: Matthew 24:3-51
Place: The Mt. of Olives (p. 66)
Event: Jesus and the 'End Times'
Meditation: God knows our future better than we know our past. Praise Him in light of that.

Day 6
Scripture: John 13-17
Place: The Upper Room (see Jerusalem, p. 63)
Event: Jesus and the 'Last Supper'
Meditation: Jesus is our Passover Lamb. Thank Him for that.

Day 5
Scripture: Matthew 26:30-46
Place: Gethsemane (see Mt. of Olives, p. 66)
Event: Jesus prayed in agony
Meditation: God's purpose was to righteously save sinners. Thank Him for that.

Day 4
Scripture: Matthew 26:57-27:30
Place: The house of Caiaphas and the Antonia Fortress (p. 110)
Event: The civil and religious trials of Jesus
Meditation: His trials demonstrate a unique difference between God and men - God forgives completely and men do not. Praise Him in light of that.

Day 3
Scripture: John 19:17-37
Place: Golgotha (see Jerusalem, p. 63)
Event: The crucifixion
Meditation: Redemption is by grace alone, through faith alone, in and because of Jesus alone. Thank Him for His sacrifice.

Day 2
Scripture: Matthew 28:1-10
Place: The tomb (see Jerusalem, p. 63)
Event: The resurrection
Meditation: A dead savior cannot save. A living One can! Praise Him in light of that.

Day 1
Scripture: Acts 1:6-11
Place: The Mt. of Olives (p. 66)
Event: The ascension of Jesus
Meditation: ... that where I am, there you may be also...Can there be a greater sign of unity between God and man than this! Praise Him in light of that.

## Section I Notes

**Section I Notes**

**Section I Notes**

## Section I Notes

# Section II: *Getting Acquainted with the Holy Land*

**The Land**

The story of Israel is the story of a Land and God's covenant with the people of that Land. A trip to Israel will help you to visualize the Land God gave to His people. There are many Scriptures that describe the Land. It is a *"good and spacious land, flowing with milk and honey,"* is just one example. (See Exodus 3:8)

When Israel was delivered from Egypt, they began a journey to the 'Promised Land.' Along the way, Moses sent out spies to investigate it. He gave them instructions to *"See what the land is like: whether the people who dwell in it are strong or weak, few or many; whether the land they dwell in is good or bad; whether the cities they inhabit are like camps or strongholds; whether the land is rich or poor; and whether there are forests there or not..."* (Numbers 13:18-20a NKJV)

Later at Mt. Horeb, God sent them away from the mountain saying, *"You have stayed at this mountain long enough. It is time to break camp and move on. Go to the hill country of the Amorites and to all the neighboring regions—the <u>Jordan Valley</u>, the <u>hill country</u>, the <u>western foothills</u>, the <u>Negev</u>, and the <u>coastal plain</u>. Go to the land of the Canaanites and to <u>Lebanon</u>, and all the way to the great Euphrates River. I am giving all this land to you!"* (Deuteronomy 1:6-8a NLT underlined emphasis mine)

The map on the next page [50] shows the topography of Israel as it relates to the emphasis above.

## Israel's Topography

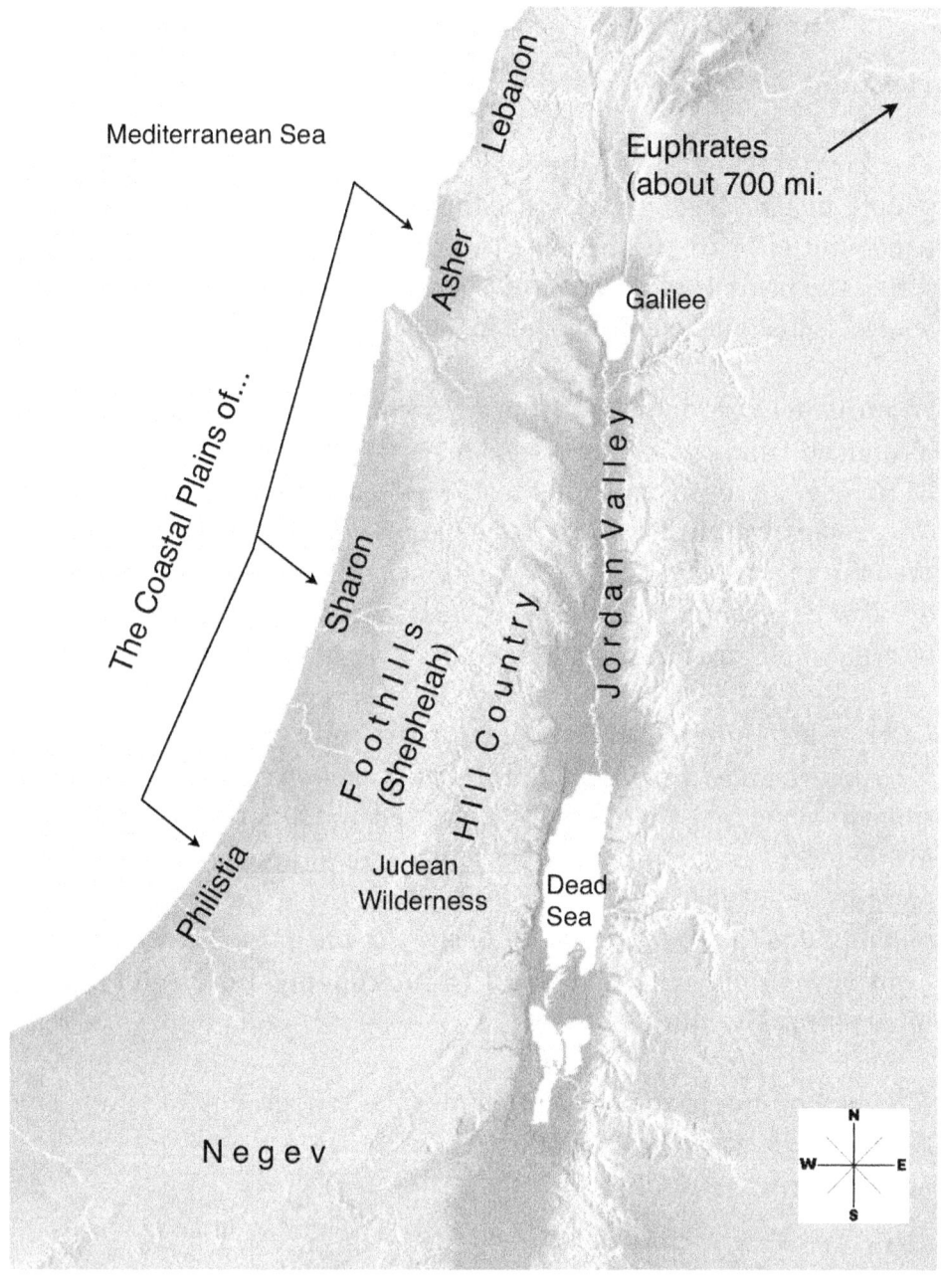

# Outline of Historical and Archaeological Periods
(Adapted from the Encyclopedia Judaica)

Note: Various sources will have differing timelines. The dates listed here are to provide approximate periods of history.

| | |
|---|---|
| 10000 -- 4000 B.C. | Neolithic Period |
| 4000 -- 3150 B.C. | Chalcolithic Period |
| 3150 -- 2900 B.C. | Early Bronze Age I |
| 2900 -- 2600 B.C. | Early Bronze Age II |
| 2600 -- 2300 B.C. | Early Bronze Age III |
| 2200 -- 1950 B.C. | Middle Bronze Age I |
| 1950 -- 1550 B.C. | Middle Bronze Age II |
| 1550 -- 1400 B.C. | Late Bronze Age I |
| 1400 -- 1200 B.C. | Late Bronze Age II |
| 1200 -- 1000 B.C. | Iron Age I |
| 1000 -- 586 B.C. | Iron Age II |

18th century B.C. - The Patriarchs: Abraham, Isaac, Jacob settle in Israel. Famine forced them to Egypt.

13th century B.C. - Exodus from Egypt, wilderness wandering, and writing of the Torah, including the 10 Commandments received at Mt. Sinai.

1050 B.C. - First Jewish Monarchy begins; Saul becomes Israel's king.

1000 B.C. - David conquered the Jebusites and made Jerusalem his capital—the City of David.

960 B.C. - First Temple Period begins with the building of the Temple by Solomon on Mt. Moriah.

930 B.C. - Israel becomes a divided kingdom; Israel to the north (10 Tribes), Judah to the south (2 Tribes).

722 B.C. - Israel crushed by the Assyrians; 10 Tribes exiled (lost in history).

586 B.C. - Judah conquered by Babylonia (Nebuchadnezzar); the first Temple destroyed, 3rd wave of exiles to Babylon.

538-515 B.C. - Jews return from Babylon and begin repairing the city of Jerusalem including the rebuilding of the Temple. Second Temple Period begins.

332 B.C. - Alexander the Great conquered the Holy Land; Hellenistic rule begins.

166-63 B.C. - Maccabean (Hasmonean) revolt against Syria (Greeks—Antiochus Epiphanes). Victory led to Jewish independence and autonomy.

63 B.C. - Jerusalem captured by the Roman General, Pompey.

63 B.C.-313 A.D. - Roman Rule

    37-4 B.C. - Herod the Great

    29-33 A.D. - Ministry of Jesus

    66 A.D. - 1st Jewish Revolt

    70 A.D. - 2nd Temple destroyed

    132 A.D. - Bar Kochba Revolt

    210 A.D. - The Mishnah completed

313-636 A.D. - Byzantine Rule

636-1099 A.D. - Arab Rule

1099-1291 A.D. - Crusader Rule

1291-1516 A.D. - Mamluk Rule

1517-1917 A.D. - Ottoman Rule

1917-1948 A.D. - British Rule after WW I

1948-present - State of Israel

To read more about Israeli history from the Jewish perspective, see www.mfa.gov.il/MFA/facts (Israeli Ministry of Foreign Affairs)

# Maps

## Middle East Today

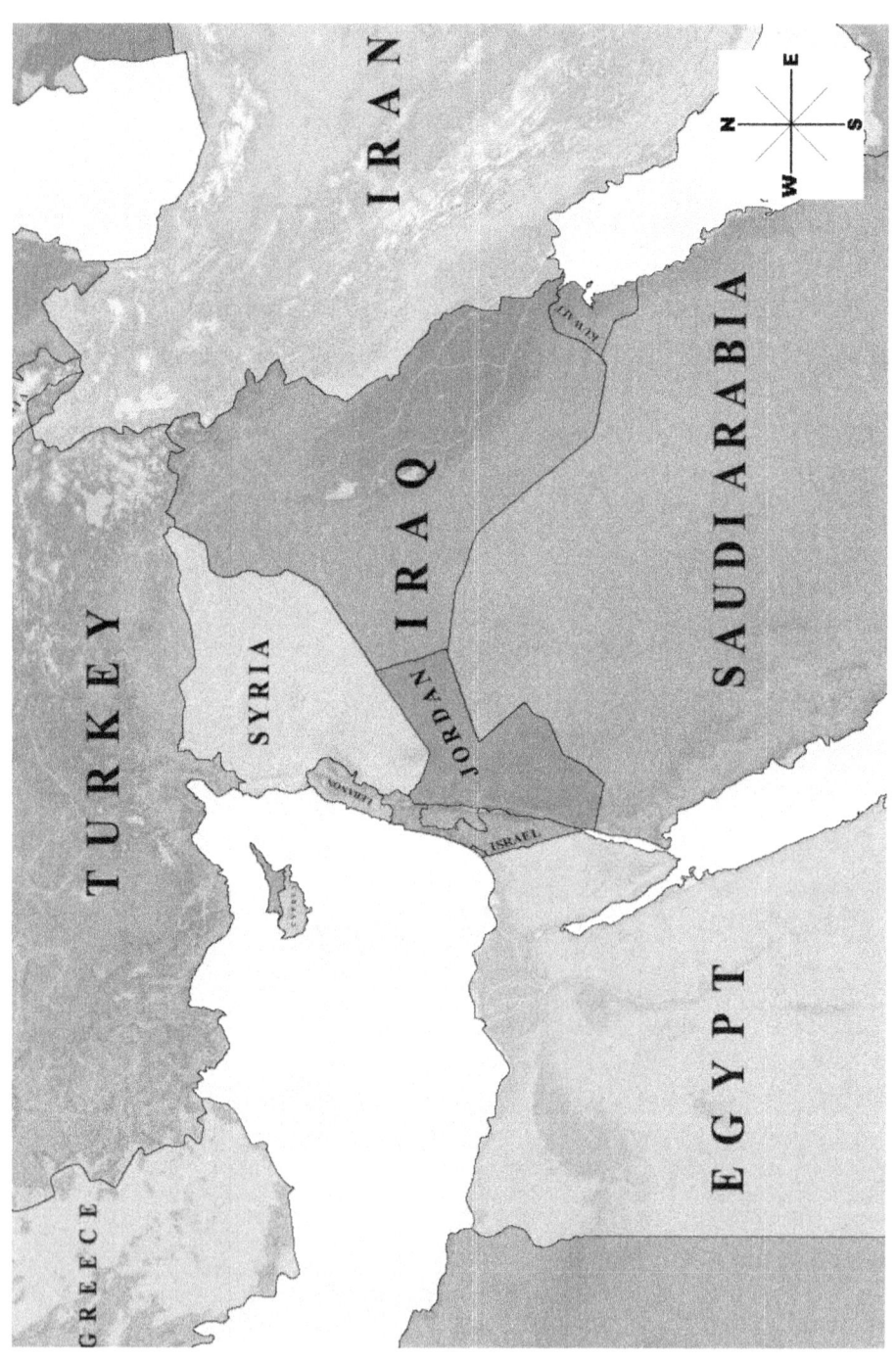

## Israel Today

# Land Allotment by Tribes
(In the days of Joshua)

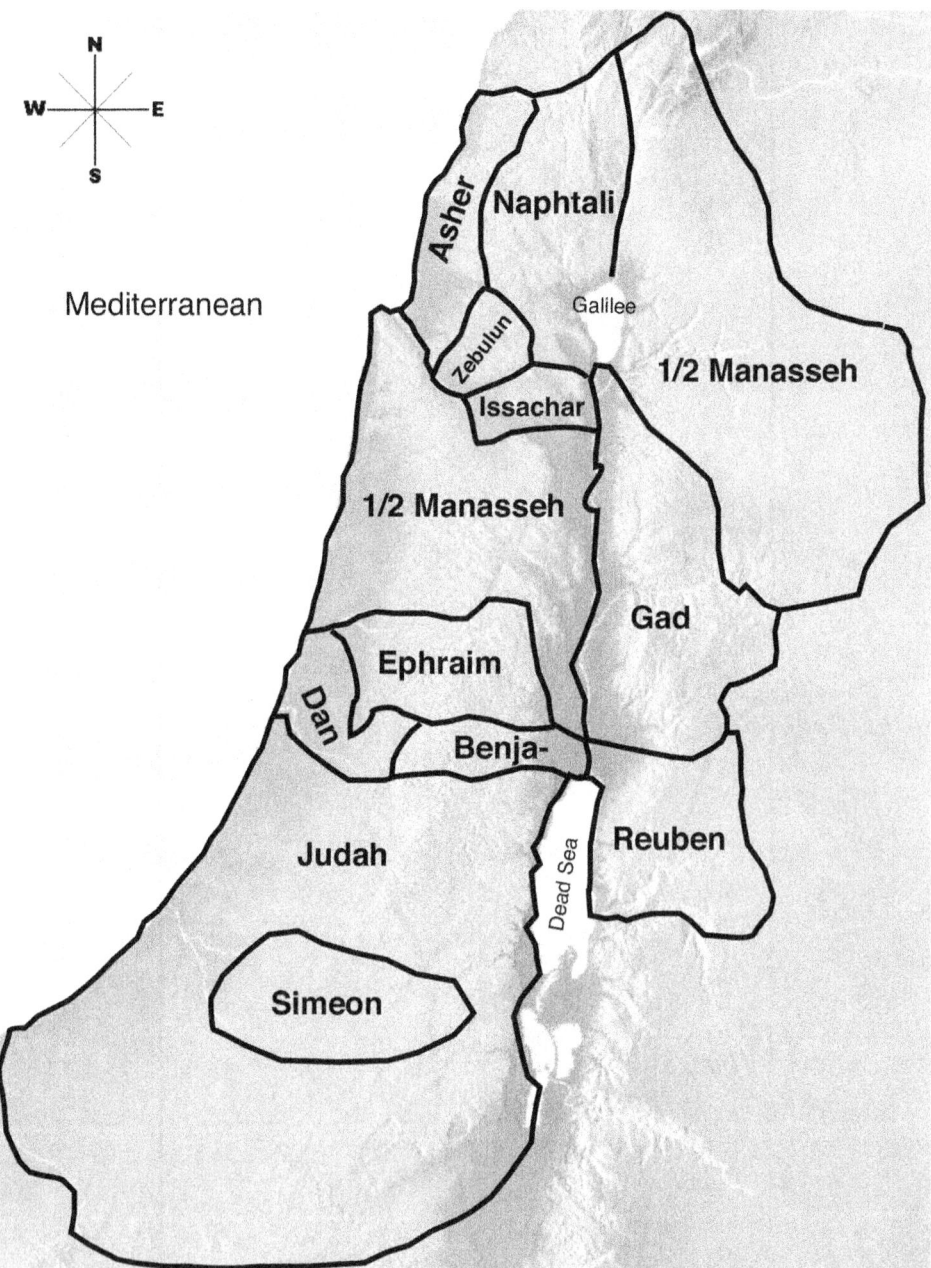

## Kingdom of David & Solomon
(the height of Israel's influence)

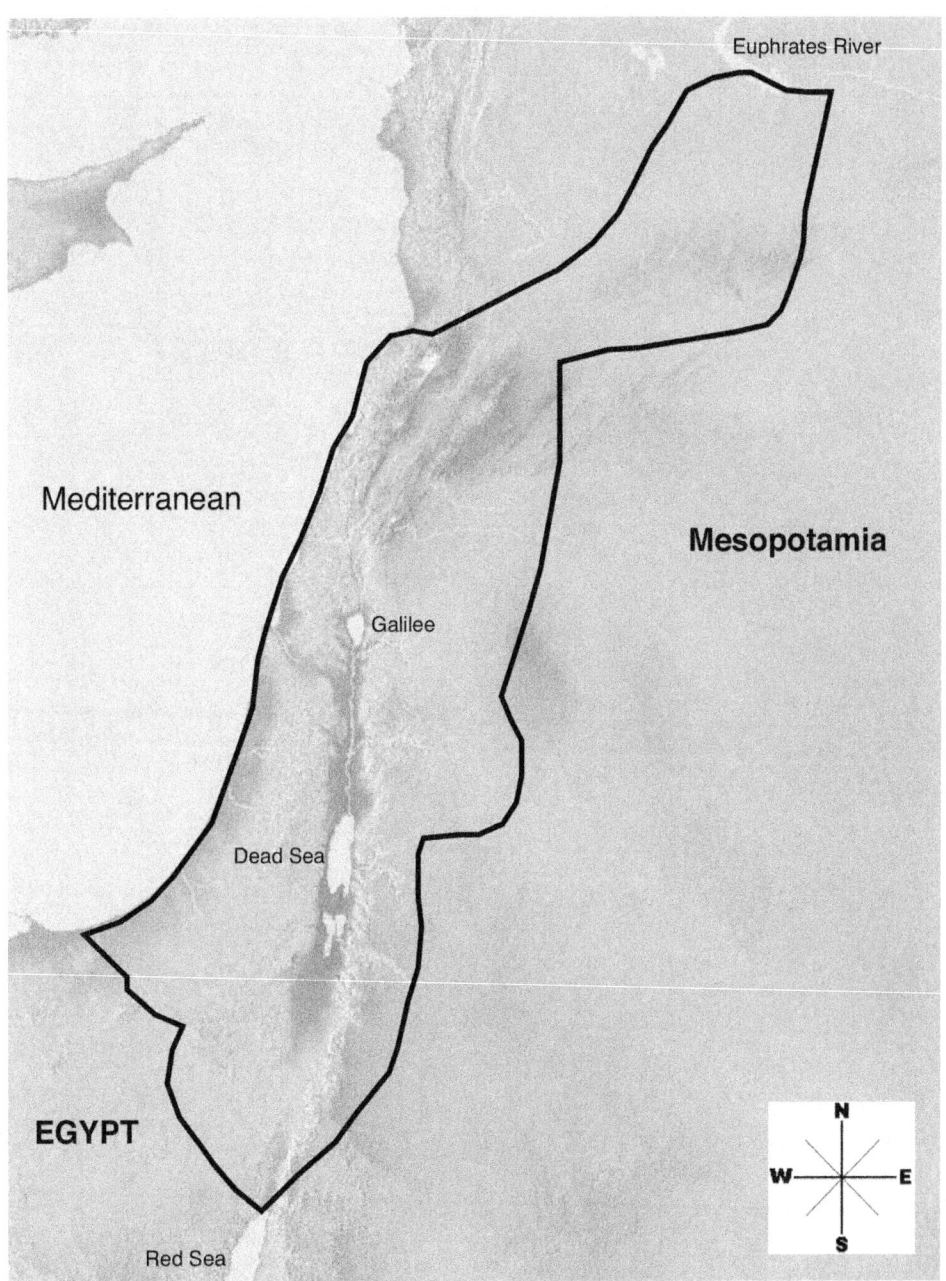

# Israel's Ancient Neighbors

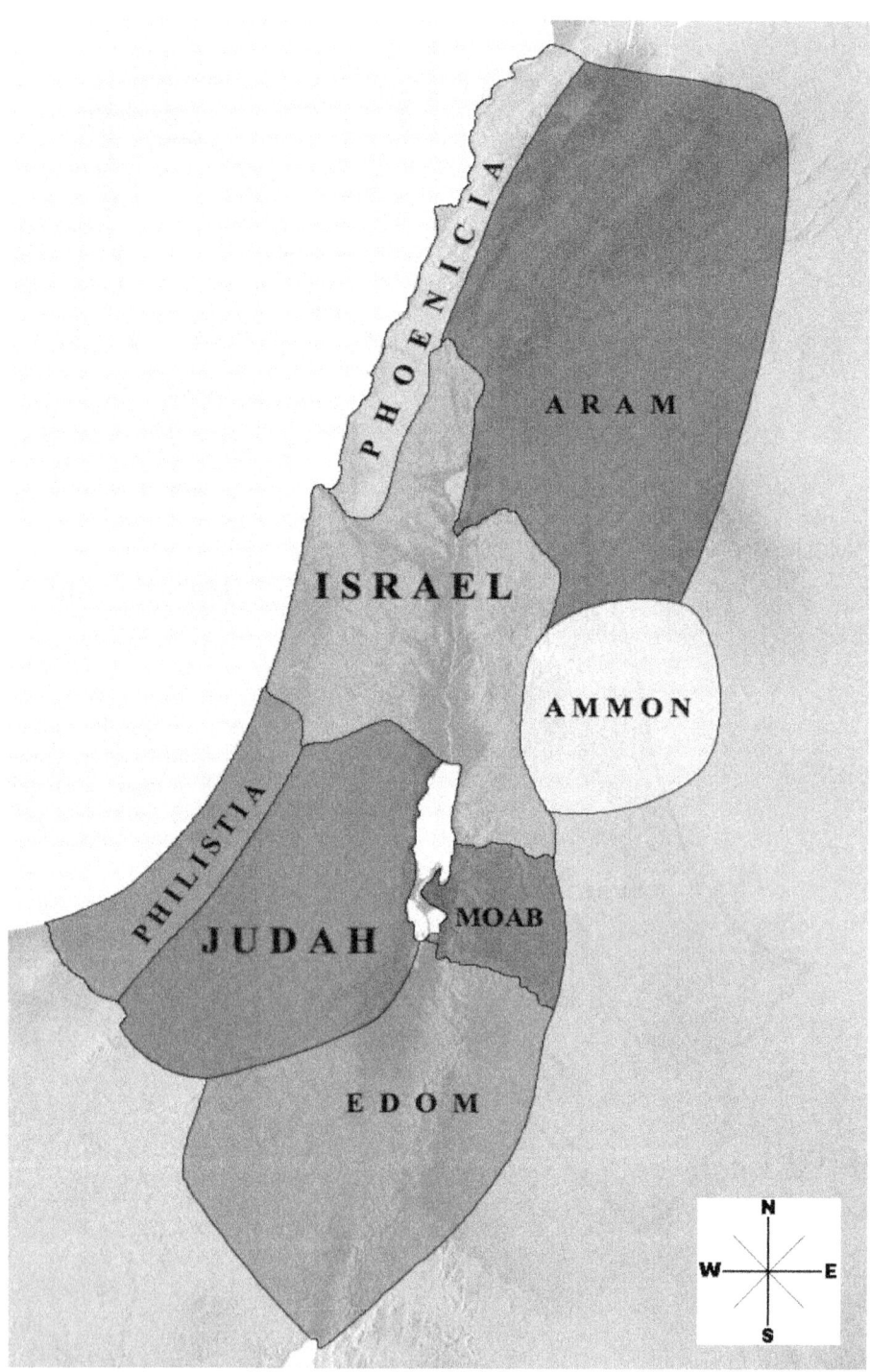

# Biblical Regions of Israel
(in modern border)

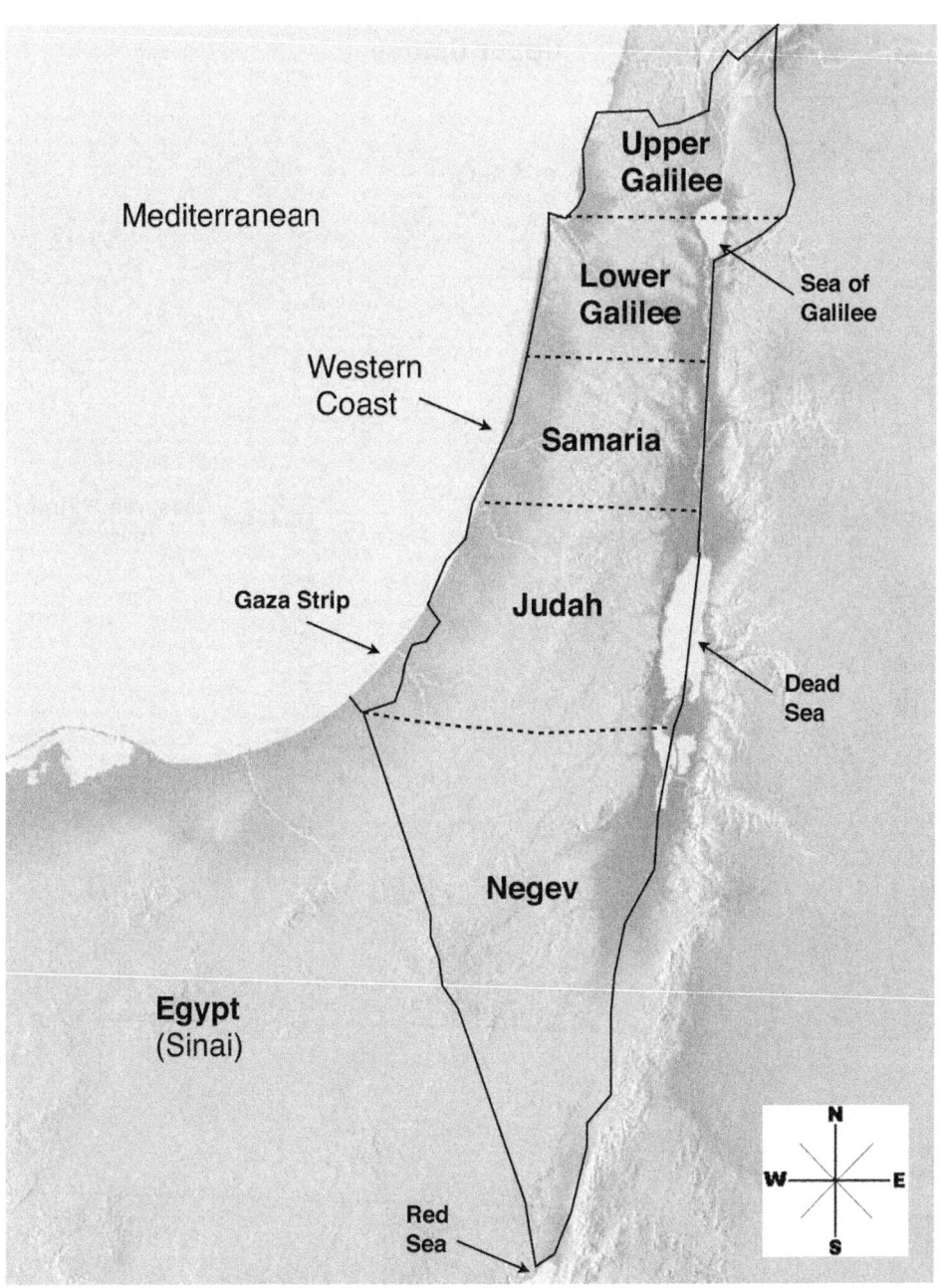

(The following 6 maps will highlight the regions shown on the **Biblical Regions of Israel** map on the previous page [59]. Starting in the north, they will move consecutively southward, with the final map showing the western Mediterranean coastline.)

## Upper Galilee

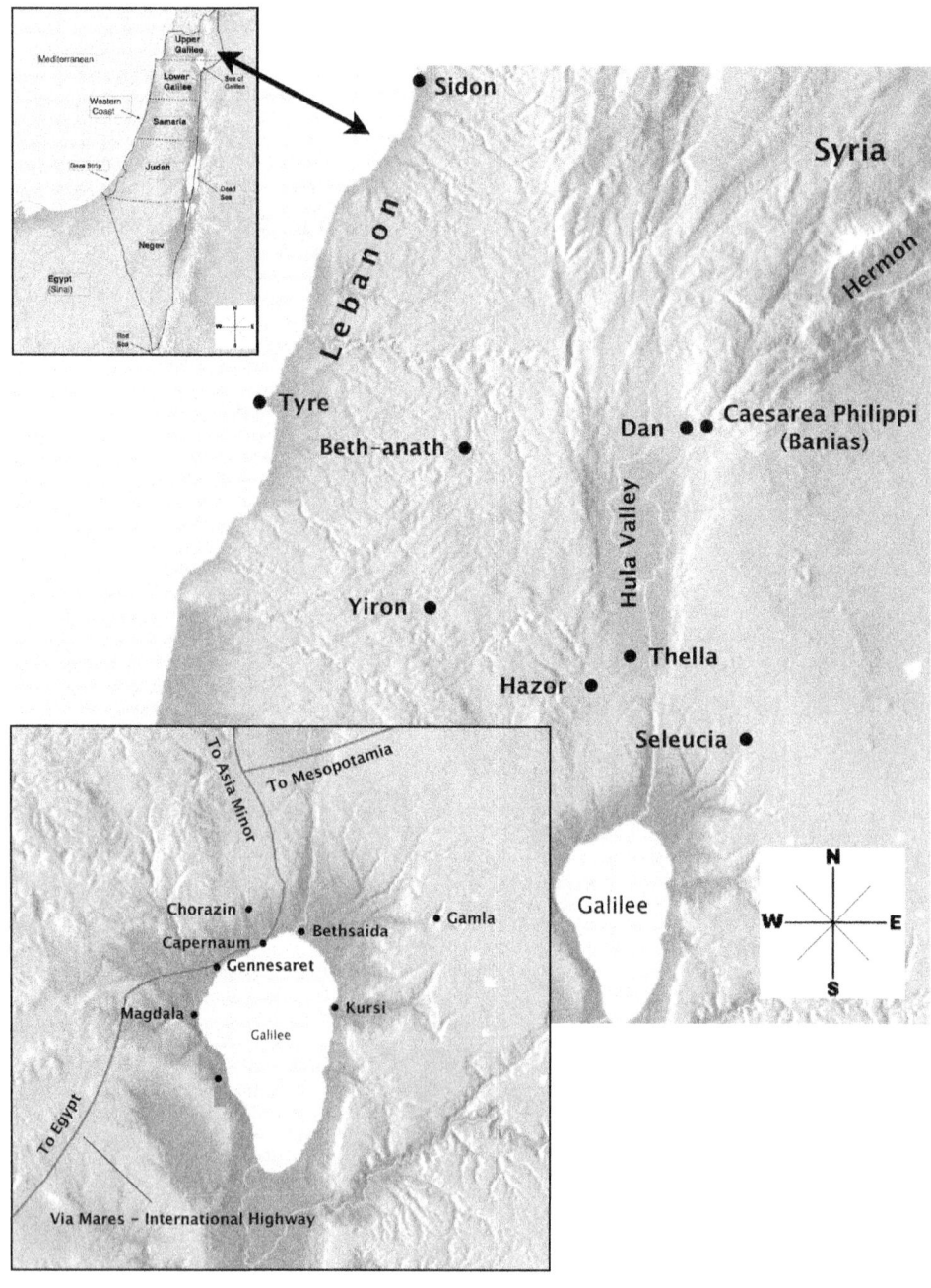

# Lower Galilee

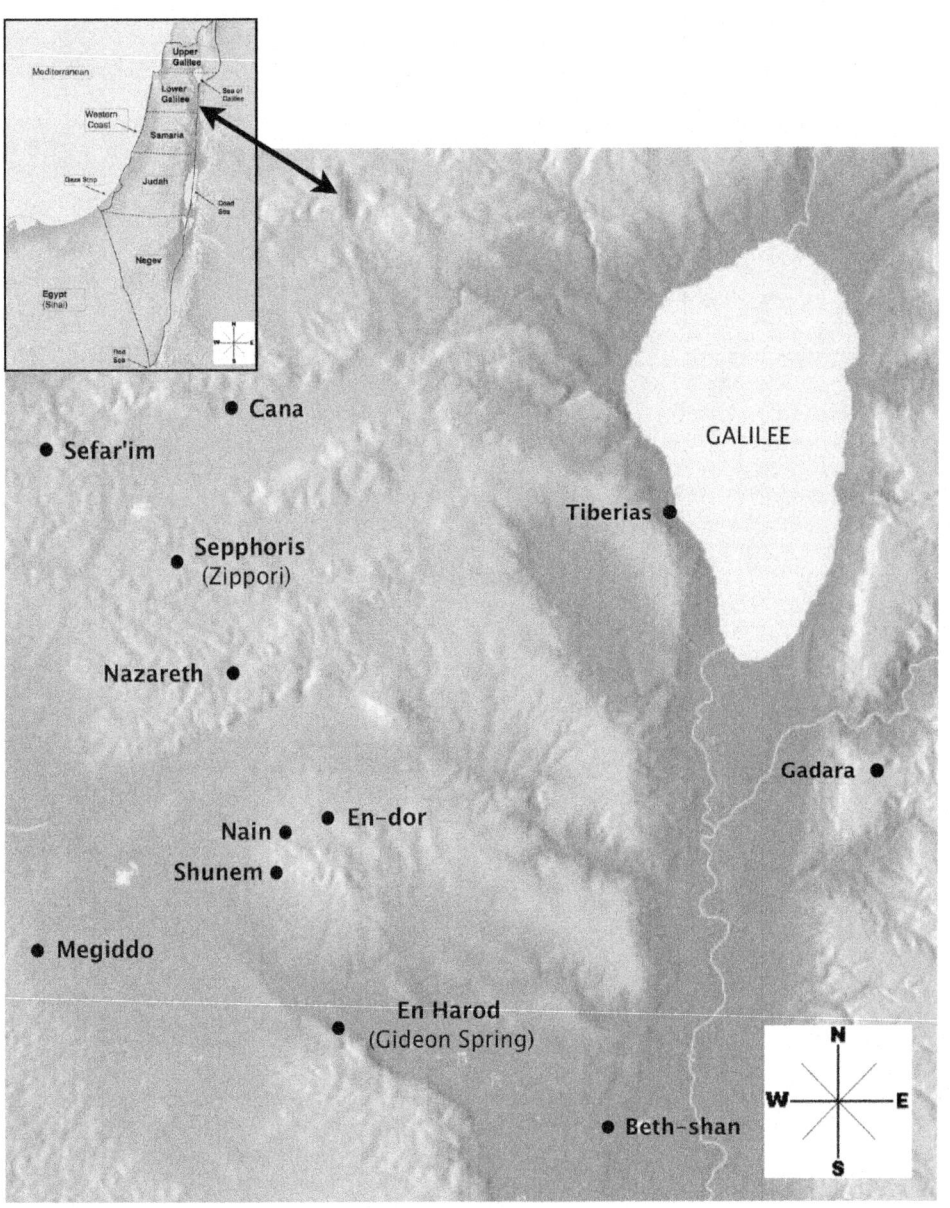

# Samaria

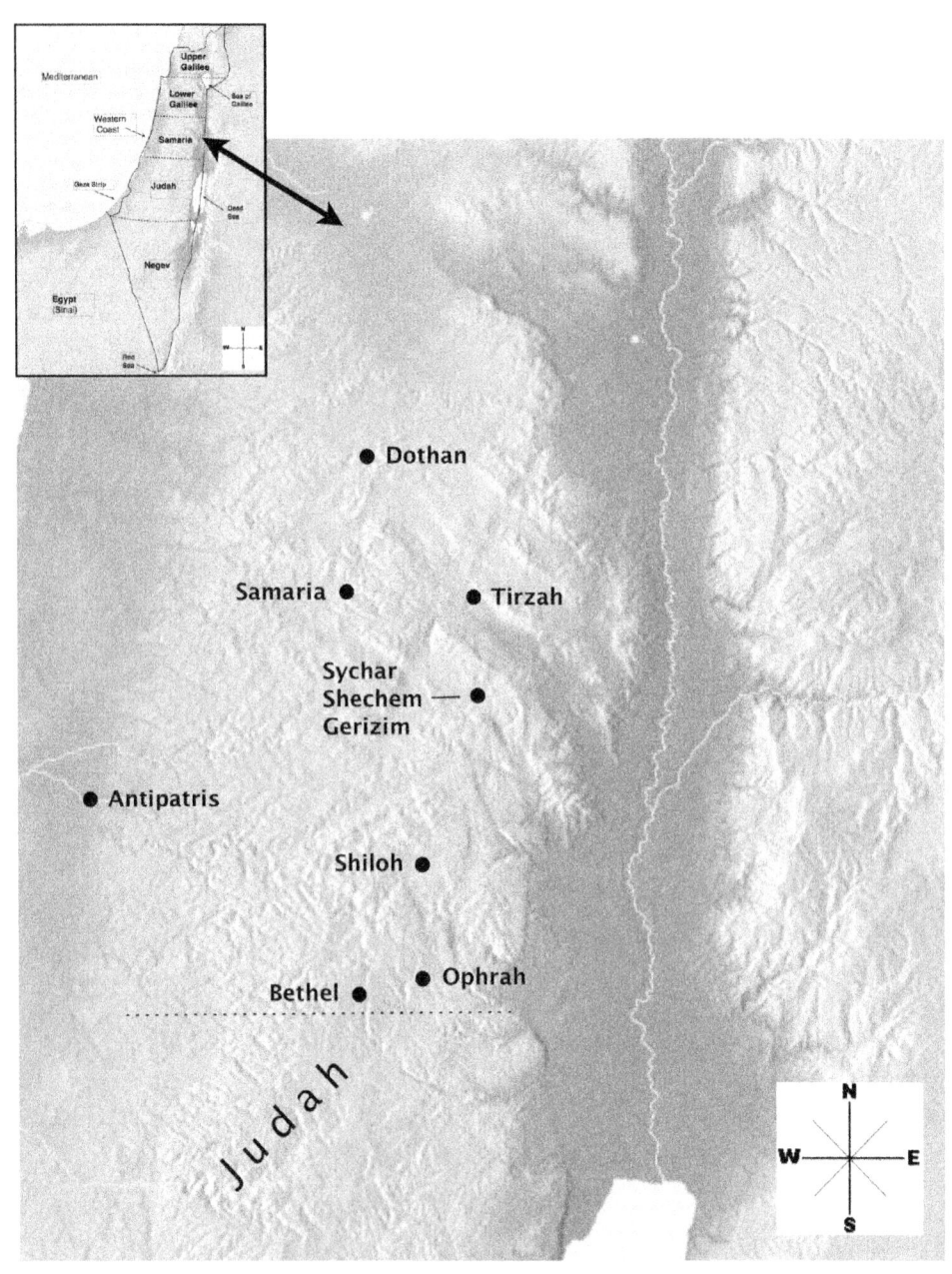

# Judah

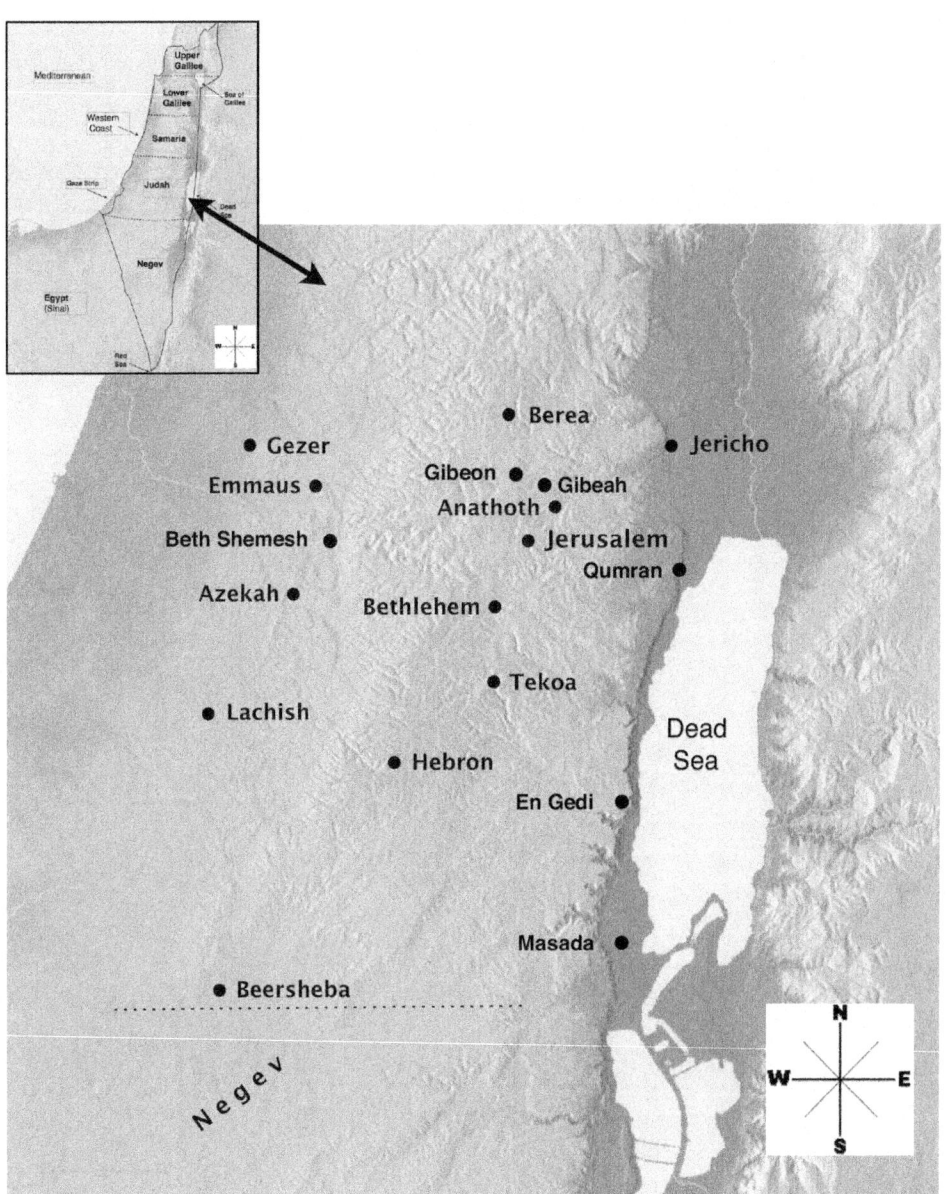

# Negev

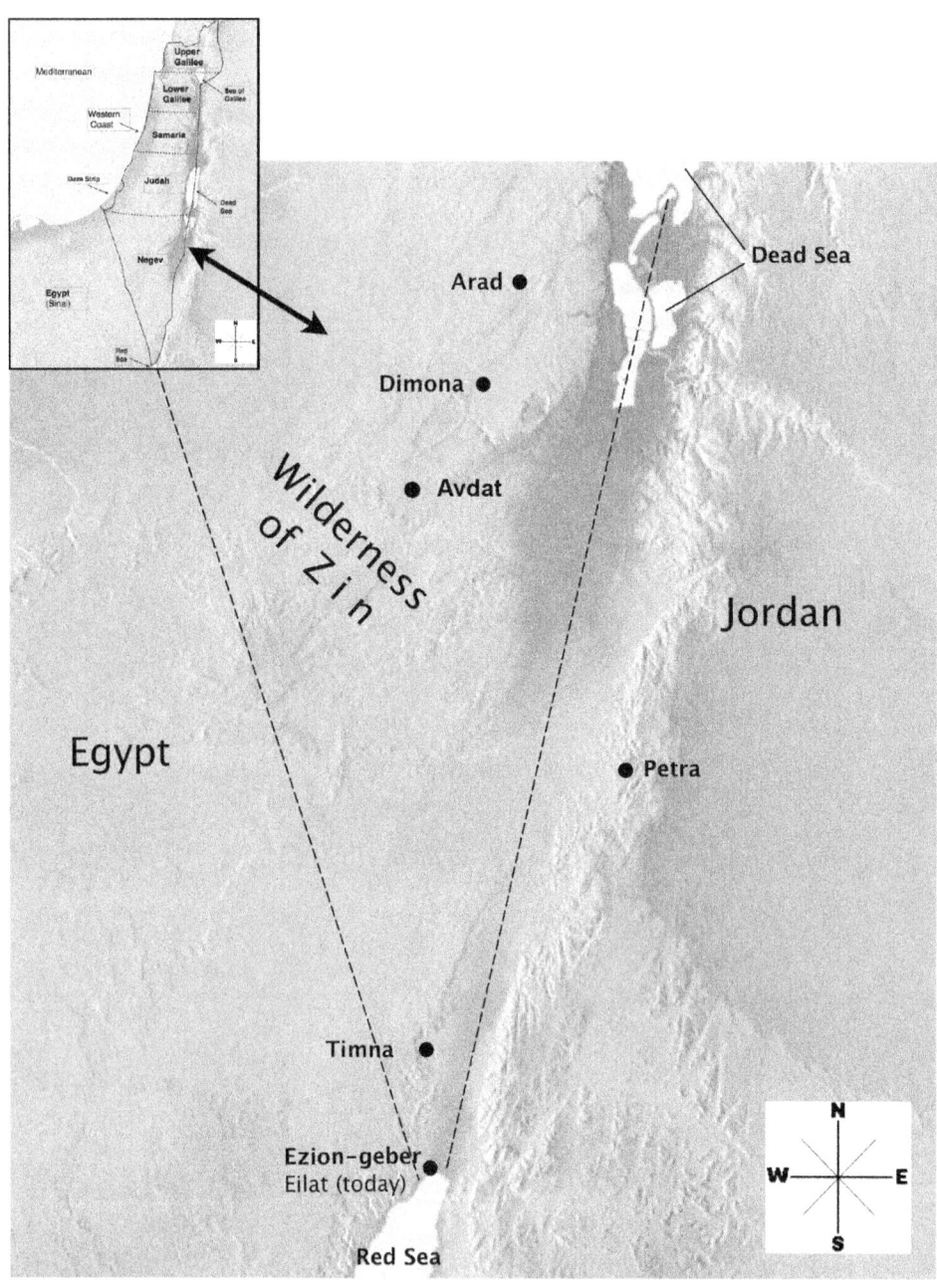

# Western (Mediterranean) Coastline

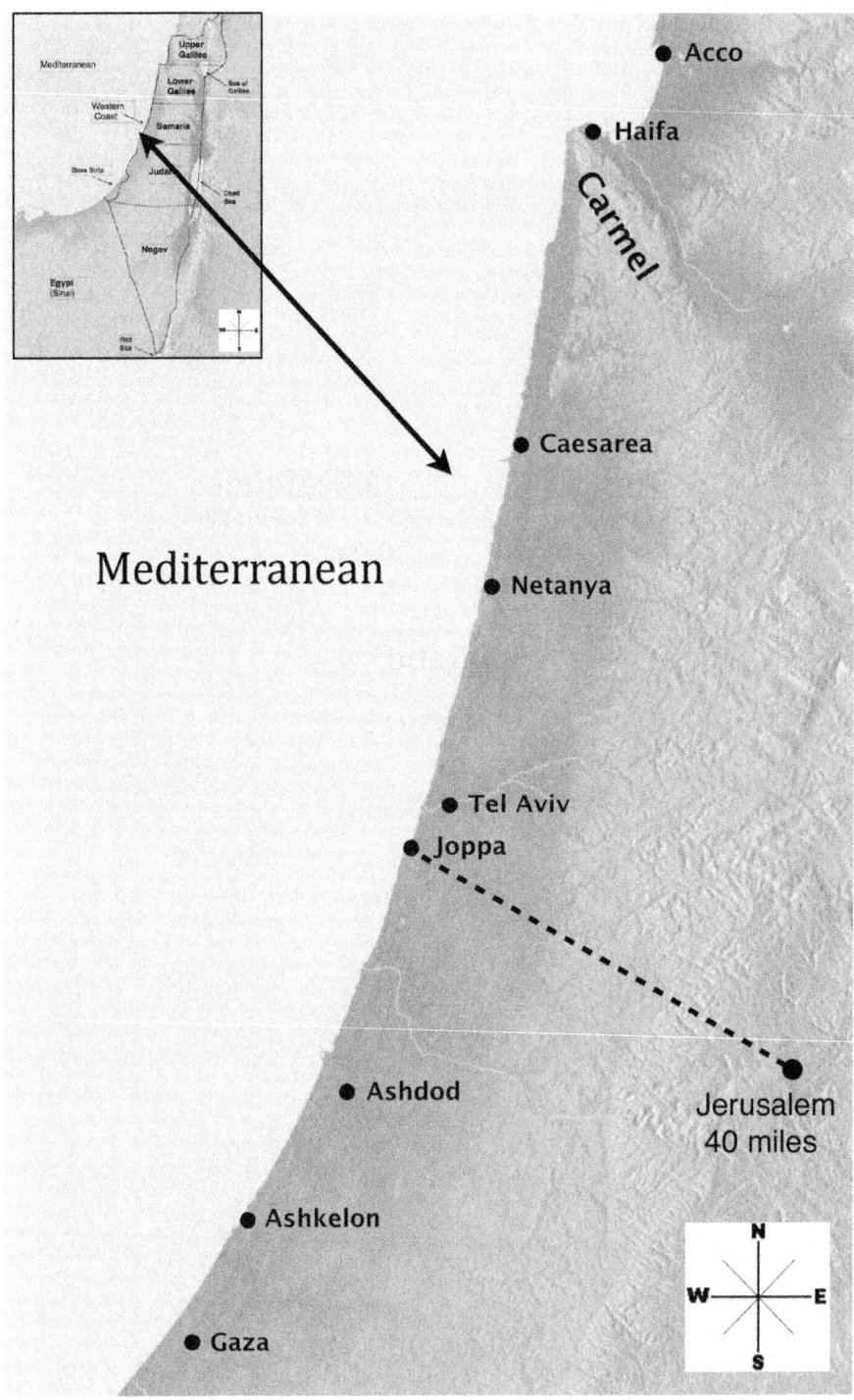

# Major Mountains in Israel

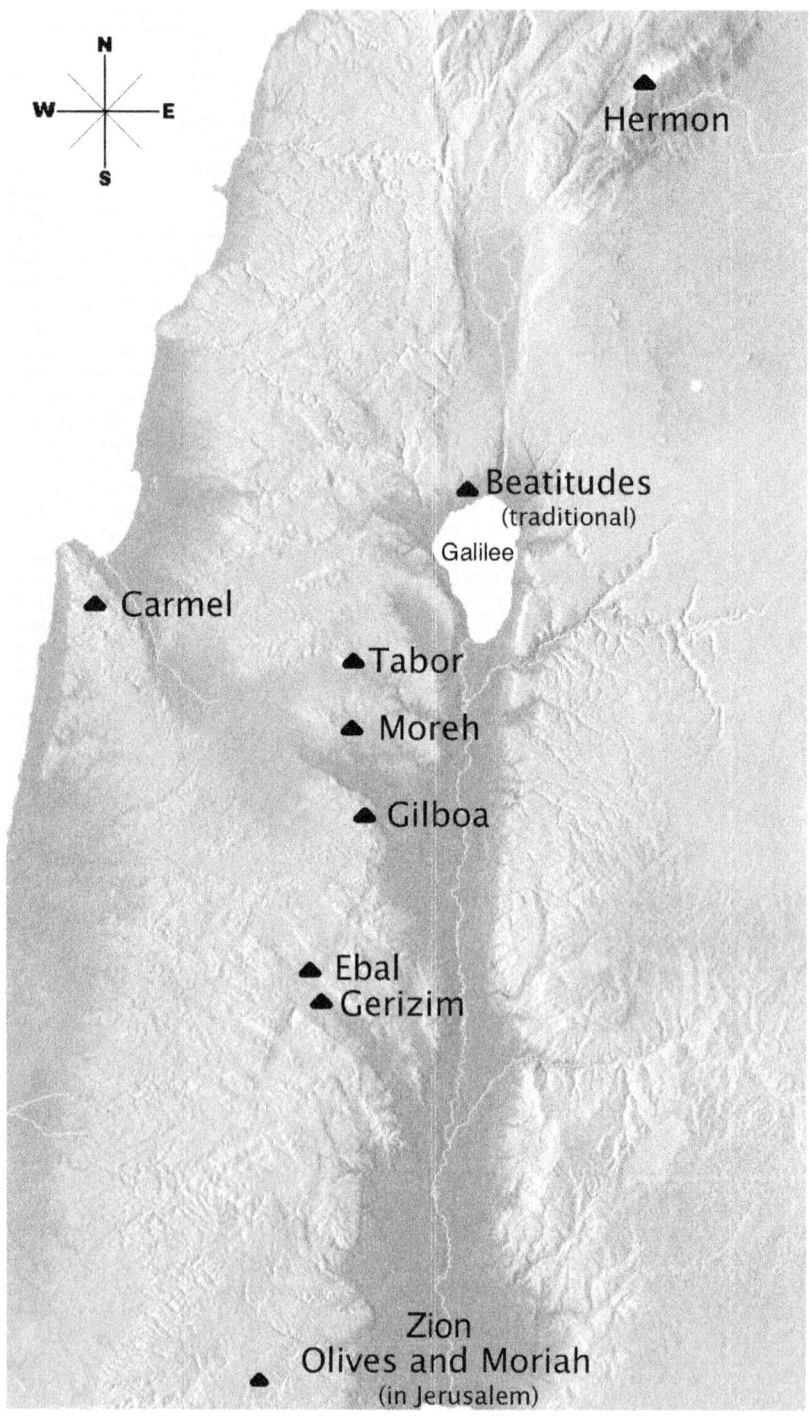

## Major Sites in Israel

Some of the sites listed below are cities and some are points of interest in a city. Where applicable, there will be a page number by the site name that will reference a map where you can find its location. I've also added additional Scriptures to some entries under the heading: References.

**ACCO**: Acre, Antiochia Ptolemais (p. 65)

The only mention of Acco in the Old Testament deals with Asher's failure to drive out its inhabitants - Judg. 1:31.

It was a major port in Israel until Herod the Great built Caesarea about 30 miles to the south.

Paul visited the city before continuing to Caesarea - Acts 21:7.

The Crusaders conquered it in 1104, and after the fall of Jerusalem, it became their last Crusader capital in the Holy Land. Marmeluke sultan, Malek El-Ashrat, conquered Acco in 1291, destroying and burying much of the city.

Later, Napoleon's troupes were stopped by the Turks at Acco in 1799.

**ALLENBY BRIDGE**

An important bridge spanning the Jordan River about 6 miles east of Jericho.

**ANTONIA FORTRESS**

The Antonia fortress was a military barracks built by Herod the Great and named after his Roman benefactor, Mark Antony. It was built on the north-western corner of the Temple Mount in Jerusalem, near the Pools of Bethesda. It is estimated that Antonia could house up to 600 soldiers. There are no remains of the fortress today.

References: Mt. 27; Mk. 15; Jn. 18:28; Lk. 23; Acts 22:22-24

**ARAD** (p. 64)

Although Arad is located in the desert, it has been repeatedly settled because it is strategically located at the crossroads of two ancient trade routes. Solomon fortified Arad to guard against Edomite aggression and marauding nomads.

It is mentioned in the list of cities defeated by Israel (Josh. 12:14) and was destroyed by Shishak - 1st Kings 14:25-28. Shishak is also known as Pharaoh Shoshenq I of Egypt.

Archaeologists have uncovered a temple in Arad, which includes an altar (the exact dimensions of the sacrificial altar in Jerusalem) and a "holy of holies". This 'high place' is believed to have been destroyed in the time of Hezekiah - 2nd Kings 18:4; 2nd Chron. 31:1.

References: Nu. 21:1-4; 33:40; Judg. 1:16

**ASHKELON** (p. 65)

One of the five major cities of the Philistines (along with Ashdod, Ekron, Gath, and Gaza), it was strategically located on the Via Mares (International Highway), the major transportation route between Egypt, Asia Minor, and Mesopotamia, thus it became an important and powerful city. Herod the Great is believed to have been born there.

After Joshua's death, Judah captured Ashkelon, but was unable to hold it - Judg. 1:18.

Samson killed thirty men, taking their clothes to pay the wedding guests who had solved his riddle - Judges 14:19.

In David's sorrow over the death of Saul and Jonathan, he asked that the tragic news not be announced in the streets of Ashkelon - 2nd Sam. 1:20.

Amos denounced Ashkelon for their sin of selling Israelites into slavery - Amos 1:8.

References: Josh. 13:1-3; 1st Sam. 6:17; and it is mentioned in the Prophets - Jer. 25:20; Zeph. 2:4, 7; Zech. 9:5

## AVDAT (p. 64)

Avdat is not mentioned by name in the Bible, but it was an important city in Israel's history. It was one of the three major cities along the Nabatean Spice Route—a caravan route that brought herbs, spices, perfumes, and other treasures from the Arabian Peninsula to Gaza by way of Petra and the Negev. It is situated on a hill about 1,900 feet above sea level in the Wilderness of Zin. After conquering Avdat, the Romans fortified it to strengthen their southern border.

In 1973, Avdat served as the location for the filming of "Jesus Christ, Superstar."

## AZEKAH (p. 63)

Azekah is nestled between the Judean Mountains to the east and the Mediterranean Sea, 12 miles to the west. It overlooks the Valley of Elah where David and Goliath had their epic battle.

Azekah was part of the camp of the Philistines fighting against Saul at the Valley of Elah - 1st Sam. 17:1.

Rehoboam fortified Azekah - 2nd Chron. 11:9 .

Nebuchadnezzar destroyed Azekah - Jer. 34:7.

References: Josh. 10:10-11; 15:35; Neh. 11:30

**BEERSHEBA**: Be'er Sheva (p. 63)

For all intents and purposes, Beersheba was the southernmost city of Israel in the Old Testament. "From Dan to Beersheba" (Judges 20:1) is how the writers of the Bible would describe Israel from north to south.

Isaac named the place his servants found water, Beersheba—"Well of the Oath" - Gen. 26:26-33.

Jacob paused at Beersheba to offer a sacrifice before leaving for Egypt - Gen. 46:1-7.

Elijah stopped at Beersheba when fleeing from Jezebel - 1st Kings 19:1-4.

References: Gen. 21:14-19, 22-33; 28:10; Josh. 15:28; 1st Sam. 8:1-2; 2nd Chron. 19:4

**BETH SHEAN**: Scythopolis (p. 61)

Beth Shean is located at a strategic junction of the Jordan and Harod Valleys just 17 miles south of the Sea of Galilee. It has been settled almost continuously throughout history, much like Jericho.

It was renamed Scythopolis between the Testaments and was known by that name in Jesus' day. It was a part of the Decapolis—a federation of ten cities united for commercial and security benefits.

Beth Shean was allotted to the tribe of Manasseh. They were unable to conquer the Canaanites because "*all the Canaanites who live in the plain have iron chariots, both those in Beth Shean and its settlements and those in the Valley of Jezreel*" - Josh. 17:16 (NIV); Judg. 1:27.

The Philistines hanged the bodies of Saul and his sons on the walls of Beth Shean after defeating them on Mt. Gilboa - 1st Sam. 31:8-12.

References: 1st Chron. 7:29; 1st Sam. 31:7; 2nd Sam. 21:12

## BETH SHEARIM

After the Bar Kochba revolt failed, Beth Shearim became one of the centers of Judaism along with Sepphoris. For a period of time, it served as the seat of the Sanhedrin.

## BETH SHEMESH (p. 63)

Meaning 'House of the Sun' and located about 12 miles west of Jerusalem, Beth Shemesh was an important city overlooking the Sorek Valley.

The Ark of the Covenant was released by the Philistines and ended up in Beth Shemesh - 1st Sam. 6:8-9, 13-20.

It is listed in Solomon's second administrative district - 1st Kings 4:9.

Shortly after the battle of Joash (King of Israel) and Amaziah (King of Judah), Beth Shemesh passed into Philistine control but was later restored under Hezekiah - 2nd Kings 14:11-13; 2nd Chron. 28:18.

Beth Shemesh was destroyed by Sennacherib, the King of Assyria, during his campaign in Judah in 701 B.C.

**BETHANY** (near Jerusalem p. 63, not shown on the map)

Located about two miles from Jerusalem on the east side of the Mount of Olives, Jesus often spent the night in Bethany on His visits to Jerusalem.

Mary, Martha, and Lazarus lived in Bethany - John 11:1.

Jesus ascended to heaven from the Mount of Olives in the vicinity of Bethany - Luke 24:50-53.

References: Mt. 21:17; 26:6: Mark 11:1; 11-12; Luke 10:38-42;19:29-40; John 1:28; 11; 12:1

**BETHEL** (p. 62)

Bethel means "house of God." It was strategically located on the main north/south road between Shechem and Beersheba. Bethel played a pivotal role in Israel's religious history.

Abraham built an altar in Bethel - Gen. 12:8.

Jacob camped at Bethel and had a vision of angels ascending and descending a heavenly staircase - Gen. 28:10-22.

Deborah held her court between Ramah and Bethel - Judg. 4:4-5.

Jeroboam set up a golden calf in Dan and Bethel. He was the first of a long line of kings that "did evil in the sight of the Lord," because he displaced Jerusalem as the place of worship - 1st Kings 12:26-33.

Bethel was a major area of Samuel's ministry - 1st Sam. 7:16.

References: Gen. 13:3; 35:8; Josh. 7:2; 8:9-12; 20:18, 26; 1st Sam.

10:3; 13:2; 1st Kings 13:1-4; 2nd Kings 2:2-3; 10:29; 23:15-19; Hosea 10: 15; Amos 3:14

## BETHLEHEM

Jacob's wife, Rachel, died giving birth to Benjamin. Her tomb is just outside of Bethlehem - Gen. 35:16-20; 48:7.

The story of Ruth and Boaz took place in and near Bethlehem.

David, born in Bethlehem, was also anointed as king of Israel there by Samuel - 1st Sam. 16:1-14; 17:12.

David was a herdsman and went from Bethlehem to the Valley of Elah where he slew Goliath - 1st Sam. 17:12-58

During his flight from king Saul, David longed for water from the well at Bethlehem 2nd Sam. 23:13-17.

Micah predicted that the Messiah would be born in Bethlehem. Fulfilling Micah's prophecy, Jesus was born there - Micah 5:2, cf. Luke 2: 1-7.

The shepherds visited Jesus in Bethlehem Luke 2:8-20.

In order to escape the cruelty of Herod, Joseph, Mary, and Jesus fled to Egypt. Herod murdered the baby boys of Bethlehem two years of age and under, attempting to kill the One born "King of the Jews" - Mt. 2:13-18.

(Photo on the left is the "Door of Humbling" on the Church of the Nativity in Bethlehem. You can see the original door lintel, but this entry was made to keep marauders from entering the church on their steeds.)

## BETHSAIDA (p. 60 insert)

Bethsaida means "house of fishing or fisherman." It was a small village east of the Jordan River and north of the Sea of Galilee. Herod the Great's son, Philip the Tetrarch, rebuilt Bethsaida and named it Julias after the daughter of Augustus Caesar.

Because Bethsaida refused to believe in Jesus as Messiah, in spite of the miracles He had performed. Jesus rebuked it along with Capernaum and Chorazin - Mt. 11:20-22.

Jesus fed over five thousand people somewhere near Bethsaida - Luke 9:10-17.

Bethsaida was the hometown of 5 disciples: Peter, Andrew, Philip, James, and John - John 1:44-50.

References: Mt. 14:13; Mk. 6:30-52; 8:22-26; Luke 10:13; Jn. 2:21-26

## CAESAREA (p. 65)

Herod the Great founded Caesarea in 22 B.C. He built the city over an ancient city named Strato's Fortress. It was the regional capital and seat of the Roman government in Palestine for hundreds of years. He named it Caesarea to honor Augustus Caesar. It was constructed so well and on such a magnificent plan that it was frequently called "Little Rome." Caesarea was the home of the Roman procurators including Pontius Pilate. While excavating the theater area in 1961, archaeologists found an inscribed stone, which bore the names of Pilate and Tiberius. Up to then, the only known reference to Pilate outside of the gospels were Josephus (Ant. 18.3.1) and a couple of Roman documents.

For some time, the city stood with varying fortunes until 1256 A.D., when the Egyptians, under Sultan Bibars, destroyed most of the city.

Philip settled in Caesarea where he had four daughters who prophesied - Acts 8:40; 21:8-9.

Responding to a vision from God in Joppa, Peter went to Caesarea and preached in the home of Cornelius. He and his household came to faith as a result, opening the gospel to the Gentiles - Acts 10.

On Paul's third visit to Caesarea, he was warned to avoid Jerusalem. The warning included being taken captive by the Jews and being delivered to the Gentiles - Acts 9:30; 18:22; 21:8-16.

During the two years Paul spent in prison in Caesarea, he made a grand defense of his ministry before Felix and Festus (Roman governors or procurators) and before King Herod Agrippa II - Acts 23:23-35.

References: Acts 12:19-23; 24 & 25; 27:1

**CAESAREA PHILIPPI**: Banias, Panias (p. 60)

Not long before Christ, Caesarea Philippi was known as Panias, so named for the worship of Pan. It got its new name when Herod Philip rebuilt the city, made it the capital of his region, and renamed it to honor Caesar. Caesarea Philippi = Philip's Caesar. Perhaps the name was to distinguish it from other cities named Caesarea, like the famous port city his father, Herod the Great, built. Some think he added his name to elevate his own reputation.

Caesarea Philippi was the northernmost limit of Christ's ministry in Israel and is the place where Peter proclaimed the deity of Jesus in response to His question, *"Who do men say that I, the Son of Man, am?"* - Mt. 16:13-26 (NKJV)

## CANA (p. 61)

Located about 3 miles from Nazareth, Cana was the site of Jesus' first miracle, turning the water into wine - John 2:1-11.

Cana was the hometown of the disciple Nathaniel - John 21:2.

## CAPERNAUM (p. 60 insert)

The name Capernaum is a Greek transliteration of the Hebrew words Kephar Nahum - "the Village of Nahum." Capernaum became a major city in the time of Christ because of its location on the Sea of Galilee. Fishing and olive processing were major industries there. It was on the Via Mares (International Highway), close to a point where it continued north to Asia Minor or turned to the east toward Mesopotamia. As a result of this, it controlled commerce, making it an ideal place for a Roman centurion and detachment of troops (Mt. 8:5-9), a customs station (Mt. 9:9), and a high officer of the king (John 4:46).

For 18-24 months, Jesus made Capernaum the center of His ministry activity - Matthew 4:13-16.

Jesus called Peter, Andrew, James, and John to be disciples near Capernaum - Mt. 4:18-22; Mark 2:13-22.

Matthew (Levi) was a tax collector for Rome. Even though he was hated by the Jews for his doing so, Jesus called him to be a disciple - Mt. 9:9-13.

Jesus ministered in a variety of ways at Capernaum. He was a teacher in the synagogue, a deliverer from unclean spirits, a healer, which inluded the healing of Peter's mother-in-law - Mark 1:21-34; Luke 4: 31-41.

MORE HEALINGS: Jesus healed the centurion's servant (the same officer who helped fund the construction of Capernaum's synagogue - Mt. 8:5-14; Luke 7:1-10.

A palsied man was let down through a roof to be healed by Jesus - Mt. 9:1-8; Mark 2:1-12; Luke 5:17-26.

Jesus raised Jairus' daughter from the dead here and also healed the woman with the issue of blood - Mt. 9:18-26; Mark 5:22-43; Luke 8: 40-56.

Two blind men and a mute demoniac were healed - Mt. 9:27-35; 12: 22-45; Mark 3:20-22; Luke 11:14-26.

Multitudes of the sick were healed in Capernaum. Most of Jesus' recorded miracles happened in and near Capernaum. Still, they did not believe in Him - Mt. 8:16-17; 9:36-38; 11:23-24.

**CHORAZIN** (p. 60 insert)

One of the three cities of the Gospel Triangle that was cursed by Jesus - Mt. 11:21-22; Luke 10:13-14.

**DAN** (p. 60)

"From Dan to Beersheba" was a way to express the length of Israel from north to south - Judg. 20:1.

In the Old Testament, Laish was taken by the tribe of Dan and renamed - Josh. 19:47; Judg. 18:1-31.

Abraham passed through Dan on his way to Damascus to rescue his nephew, Lot, from Chedorlaomer. (Gen. 14:13-16) Being wedged between the Philistines to the south and the Phoenicians to the north, the tribe of Dan was not satisfied with their inherited land, so they moved north, just a few miles from Caesarea Philippi - Judg. 18.

Jeroboam, the first king among the wicked kings of Israel, set up a golden calf in Dan (and Bethel) supplanting Jerusalem as the center of worship - 1st Kings 12:26-33.

The inhabitants of Dan (and Israel) were carried off and made captive to Assyria - 2nd Kings 15:29.

References: Deut. 34:1; 2nd Kings 10:29; 2nd Chron. 16:4; 1st Sam. 3:20 17:11; Jer. 8:16; Amos 8:14

**DEAD SEA** (p. 63)

The Dead Sea is the Earth's lowest point, about 1,370 ft below sea level. It is the deepest hyper-saline lake in the world, about 1,100 ft deep.

It is the second saltiest body of water on Earth, with a salinity of about 30%. This is about 8.6 times greater than average ocean salinity.

The Dead Sea was a place of refuge for King David (at En Gedi), one of the world's first health resorts (for Herod the Great near Masada), and it has been the supplier of products as diverse as balms for Egyptian mummification to potash for fertilizers.

In Hebrew the Dead Sea is called the Yam ha-Melakh, meaning "sea of salt" - Gen. 14:3; Nu. 34:3.

Ezekiel predicted a time when the Dead Sea would no longer be a salty sea, but rather a fresh water lake, with fish in abundance - Eze. 47:8-11.

**EILAT**: Ezion-geber, Elath (p. 64)

Eilat is a coastal city on the north end of the eastern split of the Red Sea. In the Old Testament, it served as Solomon's port city for trade with the Arabian Peninsula. He built a fleet of ships at Ezion Geber.

Eilat is in the Zin Wilderness, an area described as part of the wandering of the Children of Israel.

References: Nu. 33:35-36; Deut. 2:8; 1st Kings 9:26-28; 22:48; 2nd Chron. 8:17

**ELAH VALLEY** (See Azekah, p. 69. Tel Azekah overlooks the Elah Valley)

The Elah Valley is one of five valleys that run east to west from the hills of Judah to the coastal plain. Azekah is one of the principle towns there. It is the place of the epic battle between David and Goliath - 1st Sam. 17.

**EN GEDI** (p. 63)

En Gedi means "Spring of the Goats." After receiving death threats from king Saul, David found refuge in caves near this spring - 1st Sam. 23:29.

David was a man of integrity. Even when he had the opportunity to do so, he did not take the life of Saul - 1st Sam. 24.

It's possible that these Psalms (and perhaps others) were composed by David at En Gedi - Psalms 7; 42; 57; 142.

Solomon wrote about the vineyards of En Gedi - Song 1:14.

**EN HAROD** (p. 61)

Gideon camped at En Harod and used it as a testing ground to reduce the size of his army - Judg. 7:1-7.

Saul camped at En Harod in his battle against the Philistines - 1st Sam. 29:1.

One of David's mighty men lived at En Harod - 2nd Sam. 23:25.

**GAMLA** (p. 60 insert)

Gamla, according to the Talmud, had been a fortified city since the days of Joshua. It was the home of Yehudah of Gamla, a founder of the Zealot Movement c. 40 B.C. Yehudah's grandnephew, Eliezar ben Yair, led the last stand at Masada. Gamla was the last Jewish stronghold in Bashan (Golan) to be destroyed by Vespasian after a one-month siege in 67 A.D.

**GARDEN OF GETHSEMANE**

References: Mt. 26:30-36; Mk. 14:26-52; Lk. 22:39, 44; Jn. 18:1

**GARDEN TOMB**

References: Mt. 27:60; Mk. 16; Jn. 19:41

**GAZA** (p. 59)

Gaza is a narrow strip of land nestled against the Mediterranean, west of Be'er Sheva, and north of Egypt. Today it belongs to the Palestinians and is officially under the Palestinian National Authority and the Islamist organization, Hamas.

The main city in the Gaza Strip is Gaza, mainly populated by Muslims and a small group of Christians.

Samson met Delilah in Gaza. After his capture, the Philistines blinded Samson and imprisoned him at Gaza where he was made to work as a grain grinder - Judg. 16:1-30.

Gaza was one of the five major cities of the Philistines including: Ekron, Ashdod, Ashkelon and Gath.

References: Gen. 10:19; Josh. 10:41; 15:1-12; Judg. 1:18; 6:4; 1st Kings 4: 24; 2nd Kings 18:8; Jer. 47:1-5; Amos 1:6; Zeph. 2:4

## GEZER (p. 63)

Gezer is located on the western slopes of the Judean Hills about 18 miles from Jerusalem, midway between Jerusalem and Tel Aviv. It guarded one of the most important crossroads in ancient Israel, where the trunk road leading to Jerusalem branches off from the Via Maris (the International Highway) at the approach of the Valley of Aijalon.

Gezer was defeated by the Israelites - Josh. 10:33.

The Egyptian Pharaoh, Siamun, gave Gezer to Solomon as a dowry for his daughter - 1st Kings 9:15-17.

Gezer was destroyed soon after the death of Solomon and the division of his kingdom, during a campaign waged by Shishak, King of Egypt against King Jeroboam in 924 B.C - 1st Kings 14:25.

References: Josh. 12:6, 12; 16:1-3, 10; 21:21; 2nd Sam. 5:25

**GIBEAH** (p. 63)

Hometown of Saul, first King of Israel, and the first capital of Israel - 1st Sam. 10:26; 15:34; 1st Sam. 11:4.

Destroyed by Sennacherib in his campaign against Israel in 701 B.C. - Isaiah 10:29.

**GIBEON** (p. 63)

Gibeon was the chief city of a Gibeonite League - Josh. 9:14-17.

Hivites lived in Gibeon when it was under the control of the Israelites. They tricked Joshua into making a peace treaty with them - Josh. 9 & 10.

During the reigns of David and Solomon, the Tabernacle resided there - 1st Chron. 16:37-43; 21:28-30.

Solomon was in Gibeon when he asked the Lord for wisdom - 1st Kings 3:4-9.

**HAZOR** (p.60)

Hazor was as important to Israel in the Old Testament as Capernaum was to Israel in the New Testament. It was near the Jordan River and was strategically located on a spot where the Via Mares (International Highway) narrowed. It was a first line of defense against enemies attacking from the north.

When Joshua captured Hazor, it was, by some accounts, the largest city in the country - Judg. 4-5.

Because of its strategic location, Solomon rebuilt and fortified Hazor to secure and protect the northern approach to the land of Israel - 1st Kings 9:15.

**HEBRON**: Kiriath Arba, Mamre (p. 63)

Abraham lived in Hebron and purchased a burial cave there. He, Sarah, Isaac, Rebecca, and Jacob were buried at the cave of Machpelah. Herod the Great built a shrine over the cave, the remains of which stand today Gen. 13:18; 23:17:20; 25:8-10; 35:28-29; 49:31; 50:13.

Samson carried the city gates of Gaza to Hebron Judg. 16:1-3.

From Hebron, David ruled for seven years as king over Israel before moving the capital to Jerusalem - 2nd Sam. 5:5.

References: Gen. 35:27; 37:14; Num. 13:21-22; Josh. 20:1-7 2nd Sam. 2:1-5

## HERODION

The Herodion was the brainchild of Herod the Great, designed as a combined palace/fortress/city at the edge of the Judean desert near Bethlehem. Along with Masada and Machaerus, Herod intended it to be a place of protection and pleasure. It was reportedly built following Herod's 40 B.C. victory over his Hasmonean and Parthian enemies. Its commanding height made it virtually unassailable.

Upper Herodion was a circular fortress that included an elaborate palace. Lower Herodion was in a plain to the north and was an administrative and recreational center grouped around a large pool. Located 7.5 miles south of Jerusalem, the city sits on a hill shaped like a truncated cone that is 2486 ft above sea level.

Of Herodion it is said, "[he] spared no effort, skimped on no luxury, and shunned no expense." (www.jewishmag.com) The city has a breathtaking view of the Judean hills and the distant Moab Mountains. The Herodion was Herod's final resting place when he died in 4 B.C. His tomb was discovered in 2008, although it was found empty, presumably ravaged by marauders.

(This aerial view is from Wikipedia)

## HEZEKIAH'S WALL & TUNNEL

References:; 2nd Chron. 32

## HORNS OF HATTIN

It is an extinct volcano that rises about 1,000 ft above sea level. For some Protestants, it is the site of the Mount of Beatitudes. The Horns of Hattin are more associated with Crusaders than biblical events. Saladin defeated Guy of Lusignon where approximately 20,000 Crusaders were killed and 30,000 were taken prisoner. This defeat led to the subsequent fall of Crusader castles all over Israel and, eventually, Jerusalem.

## JERICHO (p. 63)

Archaeological excavations have shown that civilizations existed in Jericho as early as 7,500 B.C. It is one of the world's oldest cities.

Rahab hid the spies sent in by Joshua - Josh. 2.

Joshua captured Jericho after marching around it 13 times in seven days - Josh. 6.

Ahab rebuilt Jericho. In order to appease the gods, he sacrificed two of his sons to gain their favor - 1st Kings 16:30-34.

Elijah and Elisha both ministered here. Elisha made the bitter water pure - 2nd Kings 2:4-22.

Jericho was rebuilt by Herod the Great approximately 1½ miles to the south of the Old Testament Jericho. The city functioned as one of his winter palaces.

Satan tempted Jesus in the Judean wilderness. A traditional site of this event is the Mount of Temptation, very near Jericho - Mt. 4; Mark 1:12-13; Luke 4.

After climbing a sycamore tree, Zacchaeus met Jesus in Jericho - Luke 19:1-27.

On Jesus' final trip to Jerusalem, He healed blind Bartimaeus in Jericho - Mt. 20:29-34; Mark 10:46-52; Luke 18:35-43.

**JERUSALEM**: Salem, Jebus, City of David (p. 63)

Jerusalem has a long history. It is one of the most important cities in the entire world. It is an old city with a continuous history, which began around 3,000 B.C. and will continue in eternity as the New Jerusalem. It is a city "chosen by the Lord"

Melchizedek, meaning King of Righteousness, received tithes from Abraham in the city of Salem - Gen. 14:17-24.

Abraham was willing to offer Isaac on Mount Moriah, the mountain to the north of the Jerusalem in David's day. Mt. Moriah is now home to the Dome of the Rock - Gen.22.

Joshua defeated the king of Jerusalem, Adoni-Zedek - Josh. 10:1-12.

Jerusalem was known as Jebus, the city of the Jebusites - Judges 19: 10-11.

After reigning as King of Israel from Hebron for 7 years, David captured, Jebus and named Jerusalem as Israel's new capital. He reigned from Jerusalem another 33 years until about 970 B.C. It was called the "City of David - 2nd Sam. 5:5-16.

The Ark of the Covenant was brought to Jerusalem - 2nd Sam. 6:1-12.

David purchased the threshing floor from Ornan (Araunah) the Jebusite. That piece of property would later be the site where Solomon built the Temple - 2nd Sam. 24:18-25; 2nd Chron. 3:1.

David died and was buried in Jerusalem - 1st Kings 2:10.

Solomon reigned from 970-931 B.C. He was the king to build the Temple. He also enlarged the city of Jerusalem to the north. The walls he built would encompass the City of David, the Ophel, and Mt. Moriah (See map on page 66) - 1st Kings 6-9.

Shishak of Egypt, plundered Jerusalem in 926 B.C., when Rehoboam was the King of Judah - 1st Kings 14:25-28.

During Jehoran's reign, the Philistines plundered Jerusalem around 845 B.C. - 2nd Chron. 21:16-17.

During the reign of Amaziah, Israel plundered Jerusalem around 785 B.C., tearing down sections of the wall - 2nd Chron. 25:17-24.

While Hezekiah was king of Judah, Sennacherib, king of Assyria, surrounded Jerusalem (701 B.C.). Hezekiah sought Isaiah's counsel about the situation. During the night, deliverance came. An angel of the Lord slew 185,000 Assyrian troops, sparing Jerusalem from attack - 2nd Kings 18.

In 586 B.C. Nebuchadnezzar defeated Jerusalem after a 30-month siege. He sacked and burned Jerusalem and took the treasures of the Temple with him back to Babylon - 2nd Kings 25:1-21.

In 537 B.C., 50,000 Jewish exiles from Babylon returned to Jerusalem under Zerubbabel. They built the foundation of the temple in 536. It would take twenty years to rebuild the Temple - Ezra 1-6.

Under Nehemiah's leadership, the walls of Jerusalem were rebuilt around 445 B.C. When you visit the City of David today, you can see a part of the wall along the southeastern ridge of the city - Neh. 1-6.

Alexander the Great captured Jerusalem around 332 B.C. Legend has it that he spared the city when a high priest showed him the prophecies in Daniel that predicted the rise of the Grecian Empire.

In 20 B.C., Herod the Great began his remodel of the Temple. It would be a glorious structure. It was said of old that of all the glorious buildings ever built, none were as glorious as the Temple.

Mary and Joseph presented Jesus at the Temple. He would go there again at age 12 or 13, possibly for his bar mitzvah - Luke 2:22, 28, 41-52.

Jesus cleansed the temple - John 2:12-25; Luke 19:45-48.

Jesus' ministry included teaching and healing in Jerusalem - John 5: 7-10.

All the Gospels record Jesus' descent down the Mount of Olives and His triumphal entry into Jerusalem. There He would be greeted as a potentate with cries of, *"Hosanna in the highest."* - Mt. 21:1-11; Mark 11:1-11; Luke 19:28-44; John 12:12-19.

Matthew 24-25 - The Olivet Discourse, which predicted the destruction not only of the Temple, but also Jerusalem as well.

John 13-16 - The Upper Room Discourse. In that place, Jesus washed the disciples' feet and ate a final meal with them. That meal has been called the Lord's Supper or the Last Supper since early church history, and instituted the sacrament of the Communion.

In Jerusalem, Jesus was crucified, buried, and raised on the third day. His ascension took place on the Mount of Olives near Bethany - Mt. 27-28; Mark 15-16; Luke 23-24; John 19-20.

The church was born on the Day of Pentecost, probably at the southern entrance to the Temple Mount in Jerusalem - Acts 2.

On his way to the Temple, Peter healed a man. Shortly after that, Stephen was martyred in Jerusalem. A gate on the eastern wall the city of Jerusalem is named in his honor. (The Lion's Gate is also called St. Stephen's Gate, p. 116) - Acts 3:2, 11; 5:11; Acts 7.

Saul left Jerusalem and was later converted on the road to Damascus - Acts 9.

The Jerusalem Council convened here - Acts 15.

After his third missionary journey, Paul was seized by the Jews while on the Temple Mount. His arrest led to an appeal to Rome, which ultimately ended in his death (c. 57 A.D.) during the persecution of Nero - Acts 21:17-23; 23.

Jerusalem was destroyed by Titus in 70 A.D. and again by Hadrian in 135 A.D.

## JEZREEL VALLEY

The "Valley of Jezreel" was allocated to the tribe of Manasseh, but they could not control it because the inhabitants in Jezreel had *"chariots of iron"* - Josh. 17:16.

Gideon fought the Midianites in the Valley of Jezreel - Judg. 6:33; 7:1- 25.

Saul was killed by the Philistines at Gilboa in the Valley of Jezreel - 1st Sam. 29:1; 31:1-8.

A Shunammite's son was raised from the dead by the prophet Elisha. (Shunem is located at the foot of Mt. Moreh in the Jezreel Valley) - 2nd Kings 4:8-37.

## JOPPA (p. 65)

Solomon made it Judea's main port. Its importance was supplanted when Herod the Great built the port city of Caesarea just a few miles to the north - 2nd Chron. 2:16.

When Jonah wanted to flee from God, he caught a boat at Joppa bound for Tarshish to avoid going to Nineveh Jonah 1:3.

Peter was in Joppa when he had a vision, which prepared him to visit and preach the gospel to the house of Cornelius in Caesarea - Acts 9: 36.

## JORDAN RIVER

The Jordan flows in a unique cut on the eastern side of Israel in what is known as the Rift Valley. That valley runs from the north of Galilee all the way down to Lake Victoria in Africa.

The name Jordan comes from a Hebrew word that means: *to descend,* or *go down.* The name accurately fits this river. Run off from Mt. Hermon's peak (roughly 9,300 ft), flows down to the Dead Sea (roughly 1,400 ft below sea level), making it, in Bible days, one of the fastest flowing rivers in the world.

The Jordan River is one of the most frequently mentioned geographical sites in the Bible. It is mentioned 181 times in the Old Testament and 18 times in the New Testament.

Jesus was baptized by His cousin John (the Baptizer) in the Jordan River near Jericho.

References: Gen. 13:11; 32:10; Num. 22:1; 32:50-52; Deut. 4:21-22; 9:1; Josh. 3:15; 4:3; Judg. 8:4

## KURSI (p. 60 insert)

Kursi lies on the east side of the Galilee and is at the only spot where a cliff is on the shoreline of the lake. It is the only likely place where the story of the herd of pigs running off a cliff into the Sea could actually happen. The ruins of a monastery remembering that event, were excavated there in the 1970s.

Jesus delivered a man possessed by demons in Kursi - Mt. 8:28-33; Mark 5:1-20 Luke 8:26-39.

## LACHISH (p.63)

Lachish is regarded by some to be the second most important city in Judah because of its size and strategic location guarding the southern entry to Jerusalem.

The king of Lachish was one of the five Canaanite kings who fought against Joshua at Gibeon and who was killed at the cave of Makkedah - Josh. 10:23.

Lachish was assigned to the tribe of Judah - Josh. 15:21, 39.

Sennacherib attacked Lachish and sent three top officials from his court to negotiate with Hezekiah for the surrender of Jerusalem 2nd Kings 18:13-17.

Lachish was the last Judean city to fall to the army of Nebuchadnezzar before they lay siege to Jerusalem - Jer. 34:7.

Jews returning from the Babylonian captivity settled in Lachish - Neh. 11:30.

## MASADA (p. 63)

The Hebrew word for Masada is stronghold or fortress. Herod the Great built a winter fortress atop Masada and reinforced it with an 18 ft high wall. This fortress was thought to be impregnable.

Jewish Zealots fled to Masada after the destruction of Jerusalem in 70 A.D. Led by Eliezer Ben Yair, they resisted a three-year Roman assault.

Josephus records that the Romans finally broke through and entered Masada on April 15, 73 A.D. When they entered it, the Romans found that all the defenders had killed each other, except for two women and five children.

Masada is a shrine and symbol of modern Israel. When cadets graduate from Israel's military academy they swear a proud oath, "Masada shall not fall again!"

**MEGIDDO** (p. 61)

Megiddo is a large excavation site covering about 13 acres. It offers a magnificent view of the Jezreel Valley as you look to the north. Archaeologists have uncovered at least 20 civilizations, each of which is built on the top of the other - Judges 5: 19-20.

The Deborah and Barak defeated the armies of Sisera by the waters of Megiddo (Kishon River) - Judg. 5:19-20.

Megiddo was strategically located at the junction of the main east/west commercial route and the Via Mares (International Highway). Throughout history, whoever controlled this area controlled incoming and outgoing commerce and/or tax dollars. Over many millennia, battles were fought to control it. It was one of three cities Solomon fortified along with Gezer to the south and Hazor to the north, that made him a very powerful and a very rich ruler - 1st Kings 9:15; 10:26.

Megiddo was the battle-ground of Jehu and the King of Judah, Ahaziah - 2nd Kings 9.

Josiah was the last King of Judah, and a good one. In 609 B.C. he tried to prevent Pharaoh Necho from crossing the land and was killed in the process - 2nd Kings 23:29-30; 2nd Chron. 35:20-24.

The epic battle of Armageddon will be fought there. In Hebrew, Har Megiddo = Armageddon meaning, Mount of Megiddo - Rev. 16:13-16.

**MIGDOL**: Magdala, Tarichea (p. 60 insert)

Migdol was an important New Testament city on the Via Mares (International Highway). Its full name is Magdal Nunya, which means, "fish tower". The Greek name equivalent to it is Tarichea, which means "day fish".

Home of Mary Magdalene (Mary of Magdala) - Mt. 27:56, 61; 28:1.

Jesus came here after feeding 4,000 people. Later, Sadducees and Pharisees ask Him for a sign - Matthew 15:39-16:4.

**MT. OF BEATITUDES** (p. 66)

In ancient times, the Mount of Beatitudes was known as Mount Eremos. It is the site of the Sermon on the Mount, Mt. 5-7. A Catholic church now sits atop the Mt. of Beatitudes. Built in 1936, the funds were provided by Benito Mussolini.

## MT. CARMEL (p. 66)

Carmel comes from a compound Hebrew word that means, "Vineyard of God". The Carmel range runs from northwest to southeast (for about 15 miles), unlike the other mountain ranges in Israel that run from north to south. Its highest peak is just over 1,800 ft. It serves as a dividing point for the Plain of Asher (north) and the Plain of Sharon (south).

Mount Carmel is used in Scripture as a symbol of beauty, fruitfulness, majesty, and prosperity. When Carmel is referred to as languishing and whitening it indicates God's judgment on the land - Isaiah 35:2, 9; Jer. 46:18; 2nd Chron. 26:10; Song 7:5; Amos 1:2: Nahum 1:4.

Elijah had a contest with the prophets of Baal on the summit of Carmel. When God's name was vindicated by the consumption of a sacrifice, Elijah slew the prophets of Baal at the foot of Mount Carmel, at the Brook Kishon - 1st Kings 18:19-39.

Elijah prayed on the top of Mount Carmel that the 3½ year drought would end, then he ran to Jezreel, 16 miles away - 1st Kings 18:40.

## MT. EBAL (p. 66)

Ebal sits on the northern side of Shechem. It has a "twin peak," Gerizim to the south. It has been called the Mount of Cursing because the curses of God's law were read from its slopes - Deut. 11:29

## MT. GERIZIM (p. 66)

Gerizim is slightly smaller than its twin peak Mt. Ebal. It has also been called the Mount of Blessing because the blessings of God's law were recited from its slopes - Deut. 11:29.

*"...our fathers worshipped on this mountain..."*, the woman at the well told Jesus as she pointed to Mt. Gerizim - John 4:19-24.

## MT. GILBOA (p. 66)

The Gilboa range rises on the southeastern side of the Jezreel Valley. At a spring in En Harod at the base of Gilboa, Gideon pared his army down to three hundred men to fight the Midianites - Judg. 7.

In a battle with the Philistines, King Saul and his sons were killed on Mt. Gilboa. Their bodies were hung on the walls of nearby Beth Shean - 1st Sam. 28:4-5; 31:1-5.

Upon Saul's death, David wished that Mt. Gilboa would become dry and barren - 2nd Sam. 1:21.

## MT. HERMON (p. 66)

Mt. Hermon sits on the border of Israel and Syria. It has two peaks, the highest of which is about 9,300 ft. It is believed by some to be the location of the Transfiguration of Jesus. (See Mt. 17:1-9; Mark 9:2-9; Luke 9:28-37, which speak of a "high mountain").

Joshua's conquests went no farther north than Mt. Hermon - Josh. 11:3, 17; 12:1, 5; 13:5, 11.

In the Psalms, Mt. Hermon is used poetically because of its majestic beauty - Ps. 42:6; 89:12; 133:3; Song 4:8.

## MT. MOREH (p. 66)

Mt. Moreh is one of those places we know about because of its association with villages that played a significant role in biblical history. Ophrah, Shunem, Endor, and Nain are all located at the foot of Mt. Moreh.

**MT. MORIAH** (p. 66)

Mt. Moriah is mostly associated with two things: the binding of Isaac by Abraham, and the home of Solomon's Temple. It's hardly recognizable as a mountain. It is mostly the escarpment that rises above the Kidron Valley to the west. Solomon engineered it for the Temple and about 900 years later, Herod the Great expanded the Temple Mount floor to about 35 acres. The view of the Temple Mount from the Mt. of Olives is arguably the most photographed spot in Israel - Gen. 22:2; 2nd Chron. 3:1.

**MT. OF OLIVES** (p. 66)

The Mt. of Olives rises over 2,400 ft and is located across the Kidron Valley, east of Jerusalem. It has never been a part of the city but because of its geography and history, it is inseparably linked with it. Today, it is covered with graves and shrines, but in Jesus' day, it would have been covered with olive trees.

References: Judg. 4:6; 12-16; 2nd Sam:15:30; Zech. 14:4; Mt. 24:3; Mark 14:26; Luke 19:23

**MT. TABOR** (p. 66)

Mt. Tabor is located in the Jezreel Valley, northeast of Megiddo. It is associated with epic battles in the Old Testament including Deborah

& Barack and Gideon.

References: Judg. 4:6, 12-16; 8:18; Ps. 89:12

**Mt. Zion** (p, 66)

The eastern hill of Jerusalem. It was the stronghold of the Jebusites, attacked by Joab, and became the site of David's palace.

**NAZARETH** (p. 61)

Although Nazareth has existed since the Canaanite period, interestingly it is not mentioned in the Old Testament.

At Nazareth, Mary received the annunciation from the archangel Gabriel that she would be the mother of Jesus - Luke 1:26-28.

To escape Herod the Great's murderous decree in Bethlehem, Mary and Joseph, with the baby Jesus, fled to Egypt. When an angel told them it was safe, they returned, not to Bethlehem, but to Nazareth - Mt. 2:21-23.

Jesus was raised in Nazareth and His first recorded sermon was preached there. His message was not well received. He was taken out of the city to be thrown off a cliff (presumably the Mt. of Precipice). However, He managed to escape them by disappearing into the crowd - Luke 2:51-52; 4:16-30.

When Jesus returned to Nazareth on a later visit, His miracle power was limited because of the persistent unbelief of the people - Mark 6:1-6.

**POOL OF BETHESDA/POOL OF SILOAM**

Reference: John 5:1-18; 2nd Kings 20:20; Jn. 9

## QUMRAN (p.63)

The famous Dead Sea Scrolls were discovered in caves near Qumran in 1947. The Essenes who lived at Qumran were a monastic sect. It is believed that the Essenes, hearing of the approach of the Roman armies in 68 A.D., put their scrolls of the Old Testament and other writings in pottery jars and hid them, intending to return for them later.

Many of the Essenes who fled, joined with the forces that resided at Masada. They died in the mass suicide and we know nothing of them after 73 A.D.

## SAMARIA (p. 59 & 62)

The word Samaria, mentioned 109 times in the Old Testament, can mean a variety of things: a specific city, a provincial area, and the provincial capital of several empires i.e. Assyrian, Babylonian, Persian, and Seleucid empires.

After Solomon's death (c. 931 B.C.), the kingdom of Israel was divided—Judah to the south and Israel to the north. When king Omri came to power (884-873 B.C.), he created a new capital for Israel in Samaria. Samaria, from the Hebrew word Somron, means something like "castle" or "guard post".

It served as the royal court of Ahab and Jezebel. Ahab, influenced by his wife Jezebel, built an altar to Ba'al in Samaria - 1st Kings 16:29-31; 21:18; 22:9-10, 39.

It was the home of Micaiah the prophet - 1st Kings 22:9-10.

Samaria was destroyed and rebuilt many times. Herod the Great rebuilt the city in 27 B.C. and renamed it Sebaste in honor of Caesar Augustus (Sebaste is Greek for Augustus). Herod married his favorite wife, Mariamne, there. Later, he had her and two of his sons killed in Sebaste.

References: 2nd Kings 2:25; 7:1; Ezra 4:10; Micah 1:6; Jn. 4:4; Acts 8:14

## SEA OF GALILEE (p. 59-61)

Like Samaria, Galilee can mean a specific place i.e. the Sea of Galilee, or a region i.e. Upper Galilee, Lower Galilee. From an aerial point of view, the Sea of Galilee looks like the state of Illinois. While it is known as the "Sea" of Galilee, it is not a sea. It is a fresh water lake. It is nearly 14 miles long and about 8 miles wide at the northern end. It is 685 feet below sea level. It has many names in the Bible: Sea of Chinnereth (Num. 34:11; Deut. 3:17: Josh. 13:27; 19:35), the Lake of Gennesaret (Luke 5:1), the Sea of Tiberias (John 21:1), and the Sea of Galilee (Mt. 4:18; 15:29; Mark 1:16; 7:31; John 6:1).

The boundary of Israel on the east was the hills on the shore of the Sea of Chinnereth (Galilee) - Numbers 34:11 - Num. 34:11.

Jesus healed a leper at Galilee - Mt. 8:1-4.

Nature responded to Jesus' command - Mt. 8:23-27; Mark 4:35-41; Luke 8:22-25.

When Jesus cast out demons from the demoniac living in caves near Galilee, they entered into a herd of swine that ran off a cliff on its eastern shore - Mt. 8:28-34; Mark 5:1-21; Luke 8:26-40.

Jesus walked on the Sea of Galilee - Mt. 14:22-33; Mark 6:45-52; John 6:16-21.

After His resurrection, Jesus met the disciples on the northern shore of Galilee - John 21.

**SEPPHORIS** (p. 61)

Located in lower Galilee on a tall hill, Sepphoris is halfway between the Sea of Galilee and the Mediterranean Sea. It is called "The ornament of Galilee" and gets its name from the Hebrew for bird (tsipor).

Herod Antipas liked its strategic setting so much he made it his provincial capital when he was governor of Galilee. According to tradition, Zippori was the home of Mary, the mother of Jesus. In the 12th century, the Crusaders built a small watchtower and a church dedicated to Anne and Joachim, the parents of Mary. The remains of the tower still rest on the hilltop today.

Following the Bar Kochba revolt of 135 A.D., Sepphoris became the center of all Jewish spiritual and religious activity in Israel. The Rabbi who compiled the Mishnah (the Jewish oral tradition) lived there. At least 18 synagogues functioned in the city during the 3rd Century, although only one has been excavated thus far.

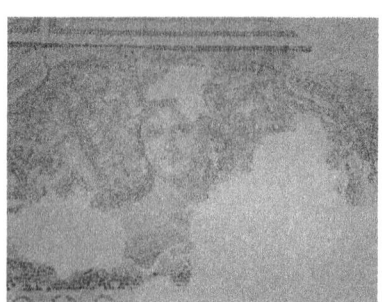

Also of interest in the city are the Roman ruins including a 4500-seat amphitheater, and a myriad of floor mosaics.

(The Mona Lisa of Sepphoris mosaic.)

## SHECHEM (p. 62)

Shechem is located in the valley between Mt. Gerizim and Mt. Ebal, about 40 miles north of Jerusalem. It is first mentioned in association with Abraham - Gen. 12:6-8).

Joseph's remains were removed from Egypt and interred in Shechem - Josh. 24:32.

Abimelech, Israel's first "unsanctioned" king, ruled from Shechem - Judg. 9:1-21.

Following the death of Solomon, Israel was summoned to Shechem to make Rehoboam the new King - 1st Kings 12:1-17, 25; 2nd Chron. 10:1-17.

Shechem no longer existed in Jesus' day, but it was the original site of Jacob's Well where Jesus spoke with the woman of Samaria - John 4: 1-42.

## SHILOH (p. 62)

Shiloh is described as a place *"to the north of Bethel, and east of the road that goes from Bethel to Shechem, and to the south of Lebonah"* (Judg. 21:19 NIV), and is located about 20 miles north of Jerusalem. Shiloh was home to the Ark of the Covenant for about 200 years.

After its conquest by Joshua, the Tabernacle of Moses was set up there - Josh. 18:1.

Eli and his sons ministered as priests in Shiloh - Judg. 18:31.

God appeared to Samuel in Shiloh - 1st Sam. 1:9; 3:1.

During a battle against the Philistines at Ebenezer, the Ark of the Covenant was brought from Shiloh into the battlefield and it fell into enemy hands. Upon hearing this, Eli fell, broke his neck, and died in Shiloh - 1st Sam. 4:1-5; 5:1.

## SOLOMON'S QUARRIES

Solomon's Quarries is located under Mt Moriah, about 30 ft beneath the Muslim quarter of the Old City. The entry is about 500 ft east of the Damascus Gate. (p. 116) It is believed by some to be the "Royal Caverns" that the Jewish historian Josephus wrote about. (War 5:147)

The quarry is about 330 ft wide and 650 ft deep, and has a hard white limestone called malaky, which Herod the Great also used in his many expansion projects.

This quarry also became known as Zedekiah's Cave. Jeremiah recorded that Zedekiah was able to escape the Babylonian siege of Jerusalem by way of a "gate" (52:7). In the account, the Babylonian

army caught up with him in the "plains of Jericho". Legend has it that David and Solomon built a series of tunnels as an exit strategy should the need arise—some as far as Jericho, 15 miles away.

References: 1st Kings 5:15-18; 6:1

## TABGHA

Tabgha is not a biblical city, but undoubtedly Jesus passed through the area. It is located about a mile and a half west of Capernaum. (See map insert on page 60) There is a church built at this location remembering the feeding of the five thousand. That event most likely did not happen there. It is, however, the likely area where Jesus met His disciples when they were fishing.

## TIBERIAS (p. 61)

The city of Tiberias was named after Tiberias Caesar, the emperor of Rome when Jesus began His public ministry. The Sea of Galilee was also known as the Sea of Tiberias. There is no biblical record of Jesus ever visiting the city. Tiberias is well known for its hot springs, which may account for why so many sick people were in the area at the time of Jesus.

Tiberias was not condemned by Jesus as was Chorazin, Bethsaida, and Capernaum. Interestingly, while they are uninhabited today, Tiberias remains a thriving city.

## TIMNA (p. 64)

About 17 miles north of Eilat, Timna Park is one of the most popular attractions in Southern Israel. Of particular interest is the life-size replica of the wilderness Tabernacle, which Moses and the Israelites built as God's dwelling place during their desert wanderings and occupation in the Promised Land.

## ZIN WILDERNESS/CANYON (p. 64)

Zin Canyon is located in the Wilderness of Zin, near where Moses' sister, Miriam, died and Moses disobeyed God by angrily striking a rock to get water for the famished people of Israel.

It is a beautiful oasis in the Negev Desert boasting eroded canyons and abundant waterfalls. It is an area frequently mentioned in the Old Testament, and is the same desert area from which the 12 spies were sent to explore the Promised Land. The Zin River was one of the historical borders of Ancient Israel.

References: Num. 13:21; 20:1; 34:3; Deut. 32:51; Josh. 15:3

# Jerusalem Supplement

## Jerusalem in the days of David c. 1,000 B.C.

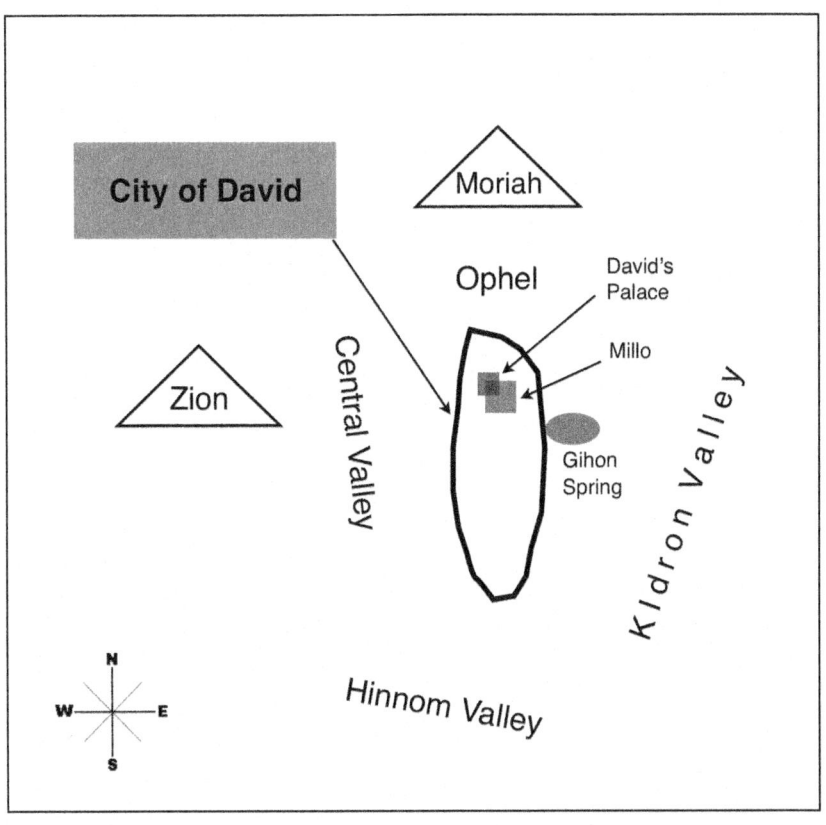

This is an artist's conception of the ancient city of David. The Millo is a Jebusite stepped stone structure—a retaining wall, mentioned in 2nd Sam. 5:9; 1st Kings 9:15; 2nd Chron. 32:5. Excavations in the City of David have uncovered this Canaanite retaining wall. Atop the Millo, the palace of David is believed to have been discovered. (See photo of the Millo below)

# Jerusalem in the days of Solomon

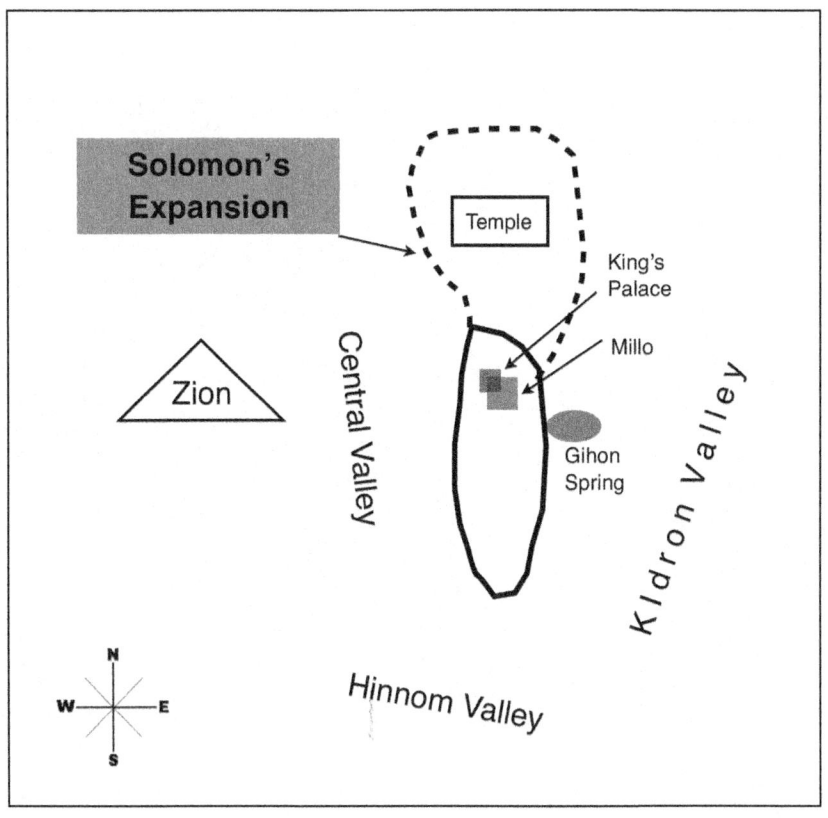

This model of Jerusalem depicts what the city would have looked like in 67 A.D. just before its destruction in 70 A.D. Geographically; you are above the Hinnom Valley in the south, looking north. I've attempted to show you where the ancient city of Jerusalem was in comparison. Some scholars suggest that David's Jerusalem might not have been larger than 20 acres before he purchased the threshing floor of Moriah. The solid line represents David's ancient core and the black outline shows Solomon's expansion. In the future, as the city continued to grow, it went to the west and north.

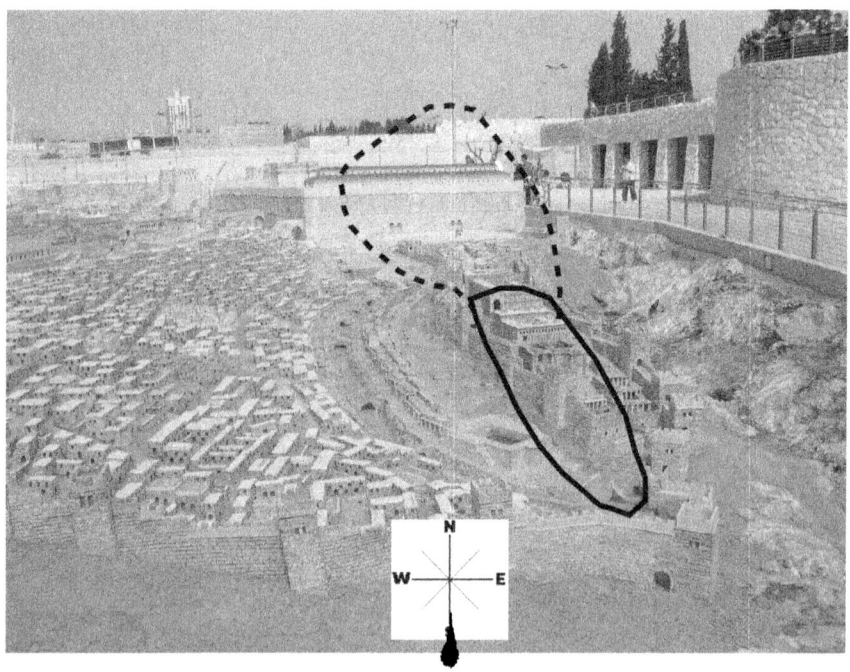

When Herod the Great remodeled the Temple, he nearly doubled the size of the Temple Mount, which is now about 35 acres.

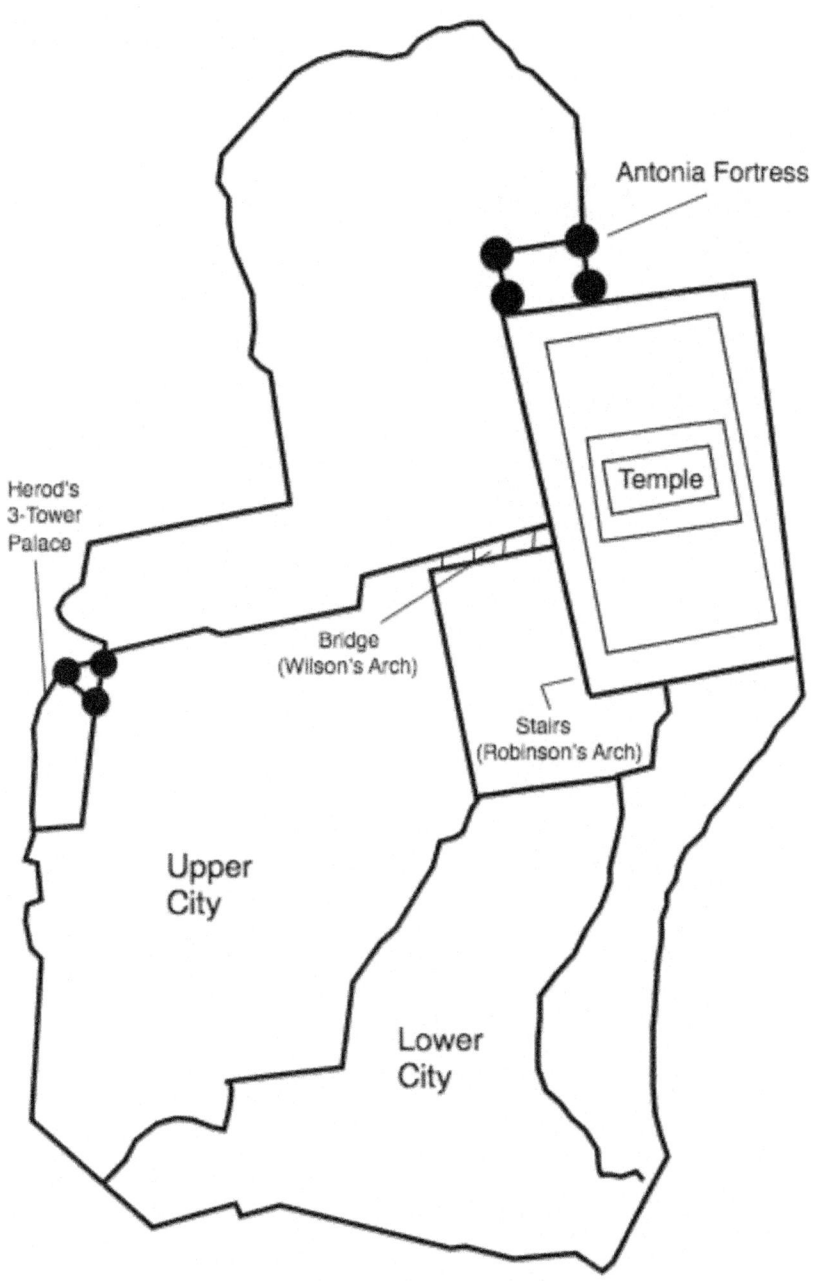

# Jerusalem in the Days of Paul

This photo taken of the Jerusalem c. 67 A.D. model at the Israeli Museum, depicts what Jerusalem was like just before its destruction by Titus in 70 A.D. Geographically, you're standing on the Mt. of Olives looking directly west. I've attempted to diagram the city from both Jesus and Paul's perspective. Jesus would not have known Agrippa's expansion, and Paul most likely did.

The Temple Mount platform was extended at least twice from Solomon's original design. The diagram below shows those expansions.

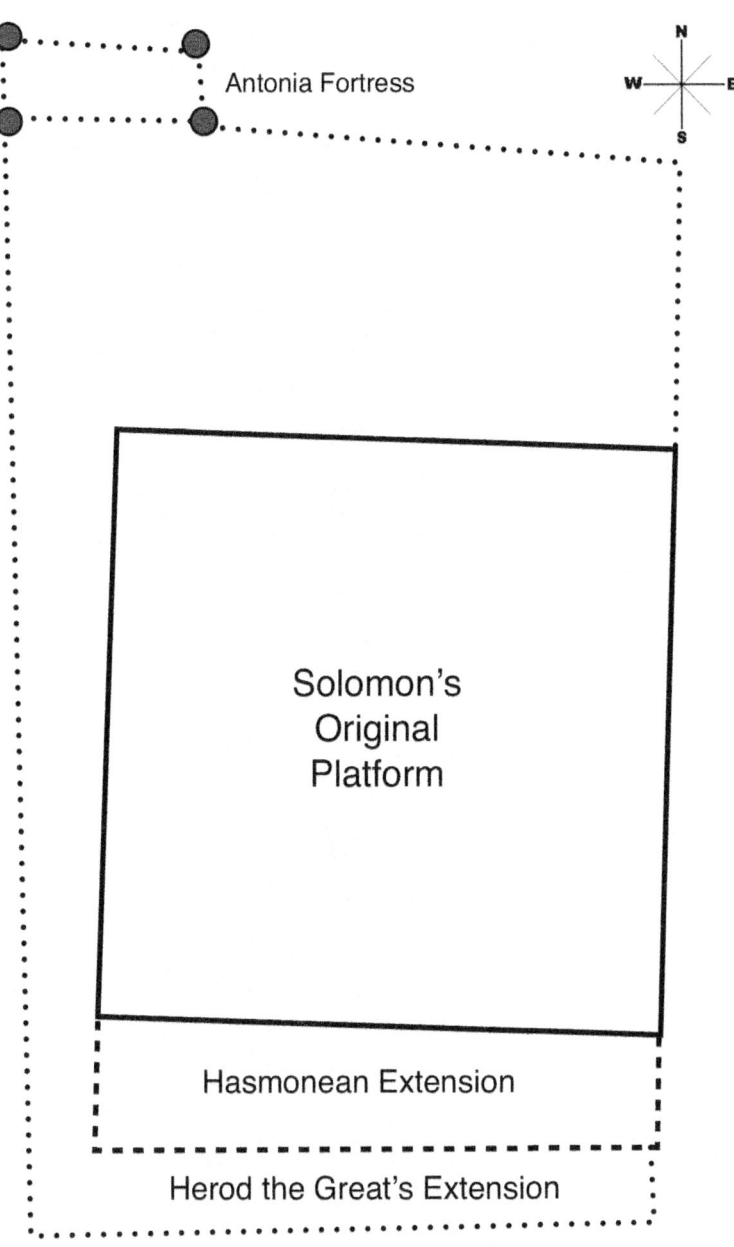

Here is a view of the eastern wall as seen from the Mount of Olives. The white lines indicate the approximate expansion of both the Hasmoneans and Herod the Great.

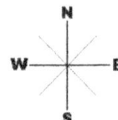

# Hadrian, the Bar Kochba Revolt, and the Decimation Jerusalem - (135 A.D.).

The 1st Jewish Revolt (that ended with the destruction of Jerusalem in 70 A.D.) failed. After that, the Romans took certain measures to prevent further uprisings. They replaced the procurator with a praetor (a commander of an army as governor) and stationed an entire legion in Jerusalem.

Still, tensions continued to build up between the Jews and Romans (Kitos War 115-117 A.D.). The 2nd Revolt, the Bar Kochba Revolt (some call it the 3rd Revolt—making the Kitos War the 2nd Revolt), ended when Rome, led by Hadrian, brought in six full divisions, and elements from six additional legions into the region.

The war lasted three years until Jerusalem was completely and brutally crushed in 135 A.D. The Jerusalem Talmud says of this war that the Romans, "went on killing until their horses were submerged in blood to their nostrils." (*Jerusalem Talmud*, Ta'anit 4:5)

According to another historian, Cassius Dio, nearly 600,000 Jews were killed in the rebellion. (roman-empire.net) Along with these staggering statistics, Hadrian set out to erase the Jewish presence from Israel.

He leveled Jerusalem and atop the rubble rebuilt a pagan city, which he named Aelia Capitolina. Aelia was Hadrian's family name and Capitolina was one of the Seven Hills of Rome on which a temple to Jupiter was located.

Jews were strictly forbidden to enter Aelia Capitolina, except on the 9th of Av, to weep as they were reminded of the ruin of their Temple on that day (perhaps how the "Wailing Wall" got its name). For the first time since David was king, Jerusalem was empty of Jews.

Below is a diagram of Aelia Capitolina, which boasted the Cardo Maximus, the main north/south street running through the heart of the city. It was also the main connection for all other streets. A secondary Maximus (Decumanus Maximus) was added later.

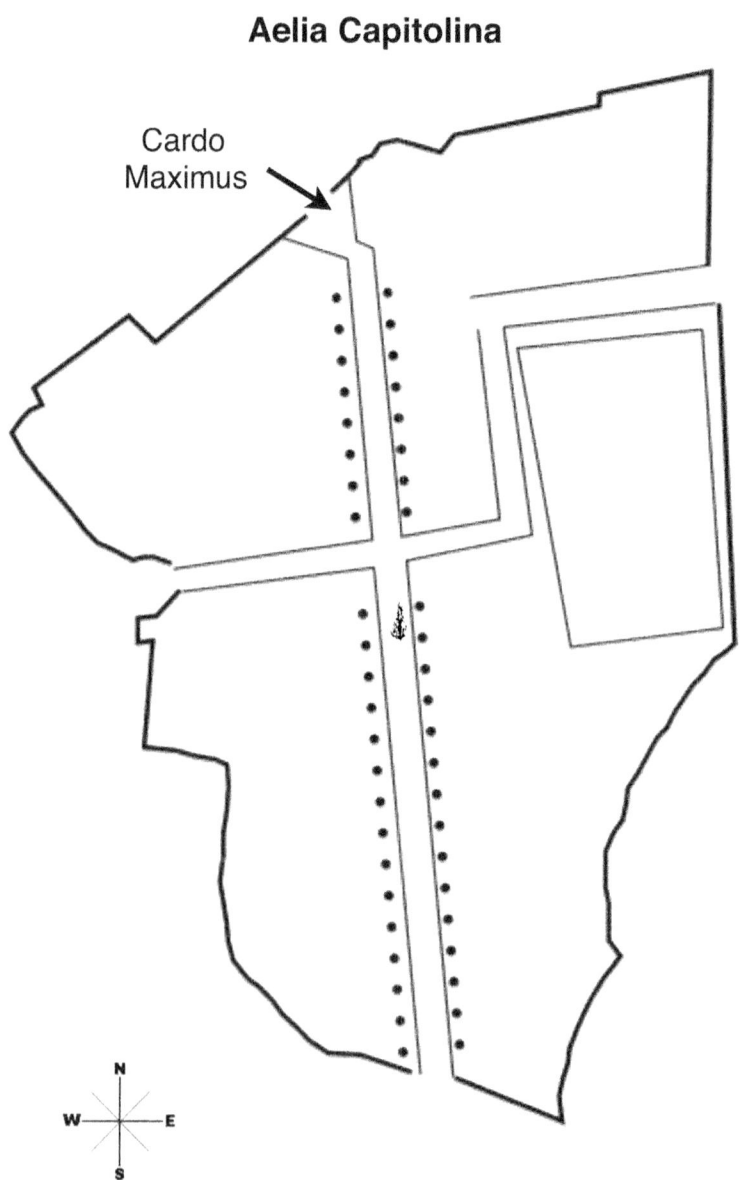

Portions of the Cardo Maximus have been excavated in the Jewish Quarter of Jerusalem. The modern street level is nearly 20 ft above the Cardo level. The staircase at the top center of the picture comes down from the modern street.

(Below) This section of the Cardo sidewalk shows two arched/vaulted storefronts.

This was a typical store along the Cardo Maximus in ancient Aelia Capitolina, the Roman Jerusalem.

A part of the ancient Cardo has been developed into an underground mall of sorts.

## Modern Wall and Gates

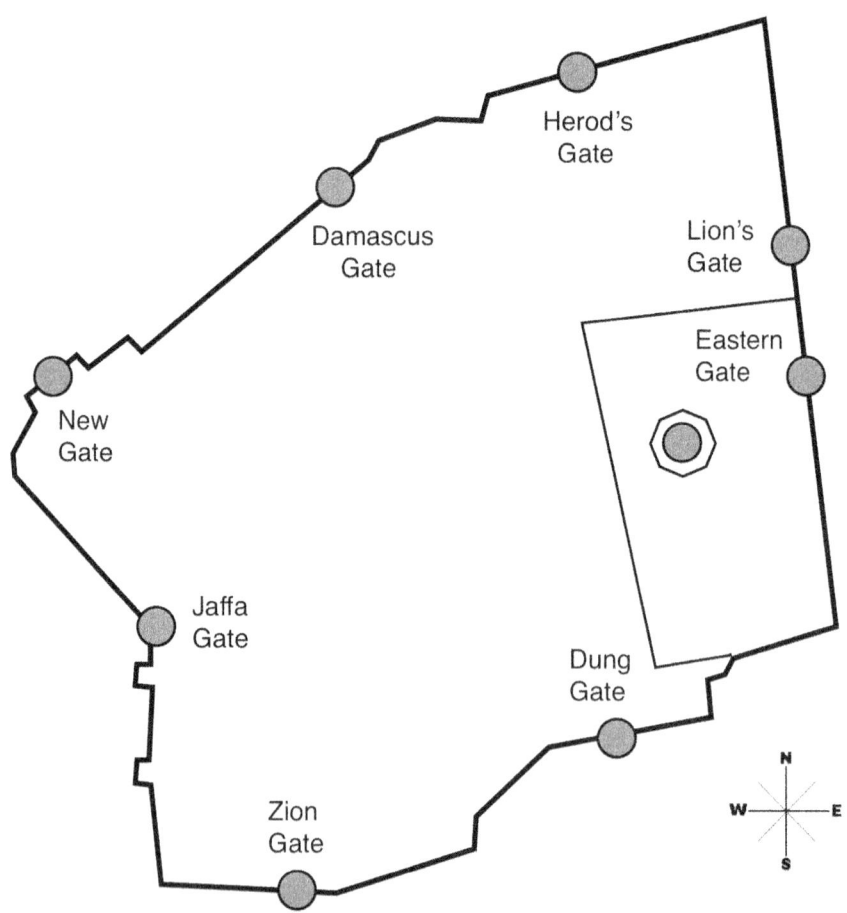

# North Wall

### New Gate

The New Gate was not part of Suleiman the Magnificent's original design in 1535 A.D. It was added to the north wall by the Ottomans in 1887. This gate offers easy access to the Church of the Holy Sepulcher.

### Damascus Gate

The Damascus Gate is the largest and most impressive of the gates in Jerusalem. It is called the Damascus Gate because the road coming out of it leads in the general direction of Damascus, Syria.

### Herod's Gate

This gate is also known as the Flowered Gate. Its name is derived from the "flower" located at the top center of the tower (indicated by the arrow). In the 1500s, Christians mistakenly believed that Herod Antipas' palace was just inside of it, hence, Herod's Gate.

# East Wall

## Lion's Gate

The Lion's Gate is so named because of the carved lions at each side of the archway (circled). The stonework with three-openings just above the arch, was used for pouring boiling oil on the enemy trying to enter the city. Originally, the gate was L-shaped. Part of it was removed so that cars could enter and exit.

## Eastern Gate

The Eastern Gate may well be the most famous of the Jerusalem gates because it has been sealed. Suleiman the Magnificent sealed it in 1541. It is also known as the Golden Gate, the Beautiful Gate, and the Gate of Mercy.

# Southern Wall

## Dung Gate

The Dung Gate got its name from refuse that was dumped here in ancient times. Nehemiah 2:13 mentions a Dung Gate close in proximity to this one.

This gate leads directly to the Western Wall Plaza and the Southern Wall Archaeological Park.

## Zion Gate

Zion Gate is located on Mt. Zion, hence its name. Its Arabic name is the *Gate of the Prophet David*. This probably came about from the misidentification of the place of David's tomb by Crusaders and other early Christians. One of the more interesting aspects of the Zion Gate is the presence of bullet damage from the war in 1948.

# Western Wall

Jaffa Gate

The Jaffa Gate got its name because the road out of it led to the port of Jaffa (Joppa). A portion of the wall between the Jaffa Gate and the Citadel of David was removed by an Ottoman Sultan in 1898 to allow Kaiser Wilhelm II to enter the city in his carriage. Between 1948 and 1967, Jordanians controlled the gate. It is the only gate on the western side of the Old City.

In total, the Old City of Jerusalem has eight gates. Six of the gates were designed with an L-shaped entry. By making a sharp ninety-degree turn, an invading army would have been slowed down in the last moments of a siege.

## Israel Notes

## Israel Notes

## Israel Notes

# Israel Notes

## Israel Notes

## Israel Notes

# Jordan Supplement

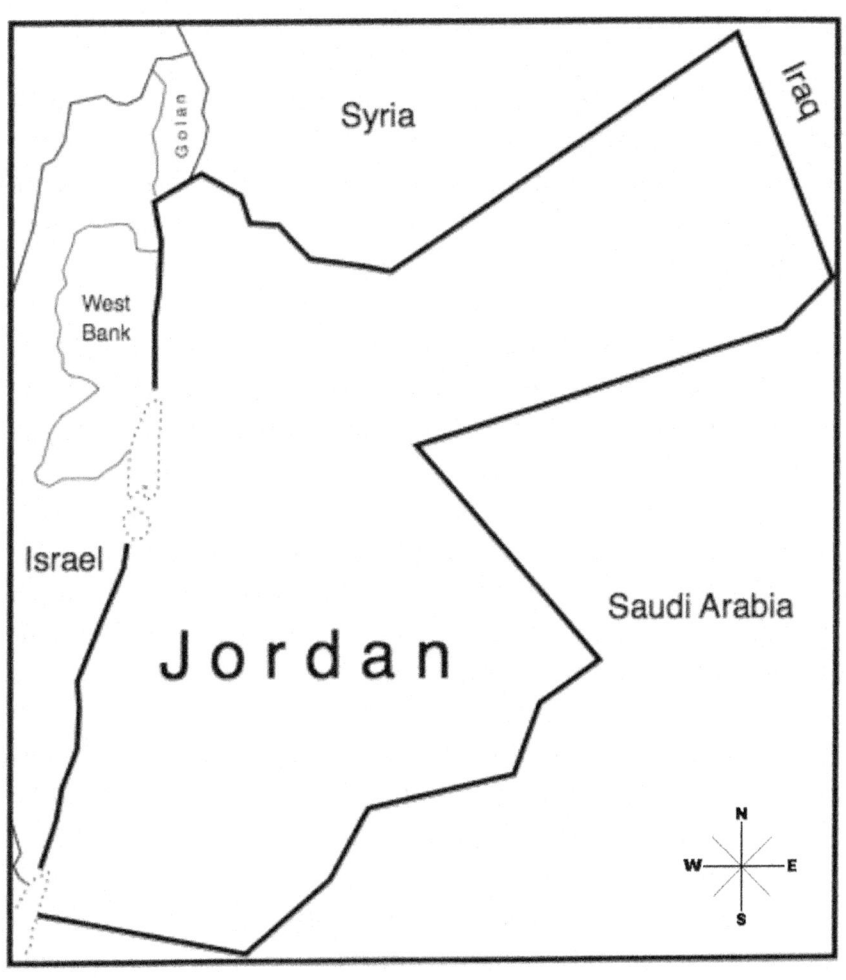

(see p. 54)

# Brief History of Jordan

Jordan, officially the Hashemite Kingdom of Jordan, is an Arab country in the Middle East in western Asia. It is bordered by Syria to the north, Iraq to the northeast, Saudi Arabia to the east and south, and Israel to the west. It shares with Israel the coastlines of the Dead Sea, and the Gulf of Aqaba with Israel, Saudi Arabia, and Egypt.

With the break-up of the Ottoman Empire at the end of World War I, the League of Nations created the French Mandate, Syria, and British Mandate, Palestine. Approximately 80% of the British Mandate Palestine was east of the Jordan River and was known as "Transjordan".

In 1921, the British gave semi-autonomous control of Transjordan to the future Abdullah I of Jordan, from the Hashemite family, who had lost their civil war with the House of Saud for control of Mecca and Medina.

In 1946, the British requested that the United Nations approve an end to British Mandate rule in Transjordan. Following this approval, the Jordanian Parliament proclaimed King Abdullah the first ruler of the Hashemite Kingdom of Jordan.

In 1950, Transjordan annexed the West Bank, which had been under its control since the armistice that followed the 1948 Arab-Israeli war. The annexation was recognized only by Great Britain.

Abdullah I was assassinated in 1951 but the Hashemites continued to rule Transjordan under British supervision until after World War I.

In 1965, there was an exchange of land between Saudi Arabia and Jordan. Jordan gave up a relatively large area of inland desert in return for a small piece of seashore near Aqaba.

# Map of Major Sites in Jordan

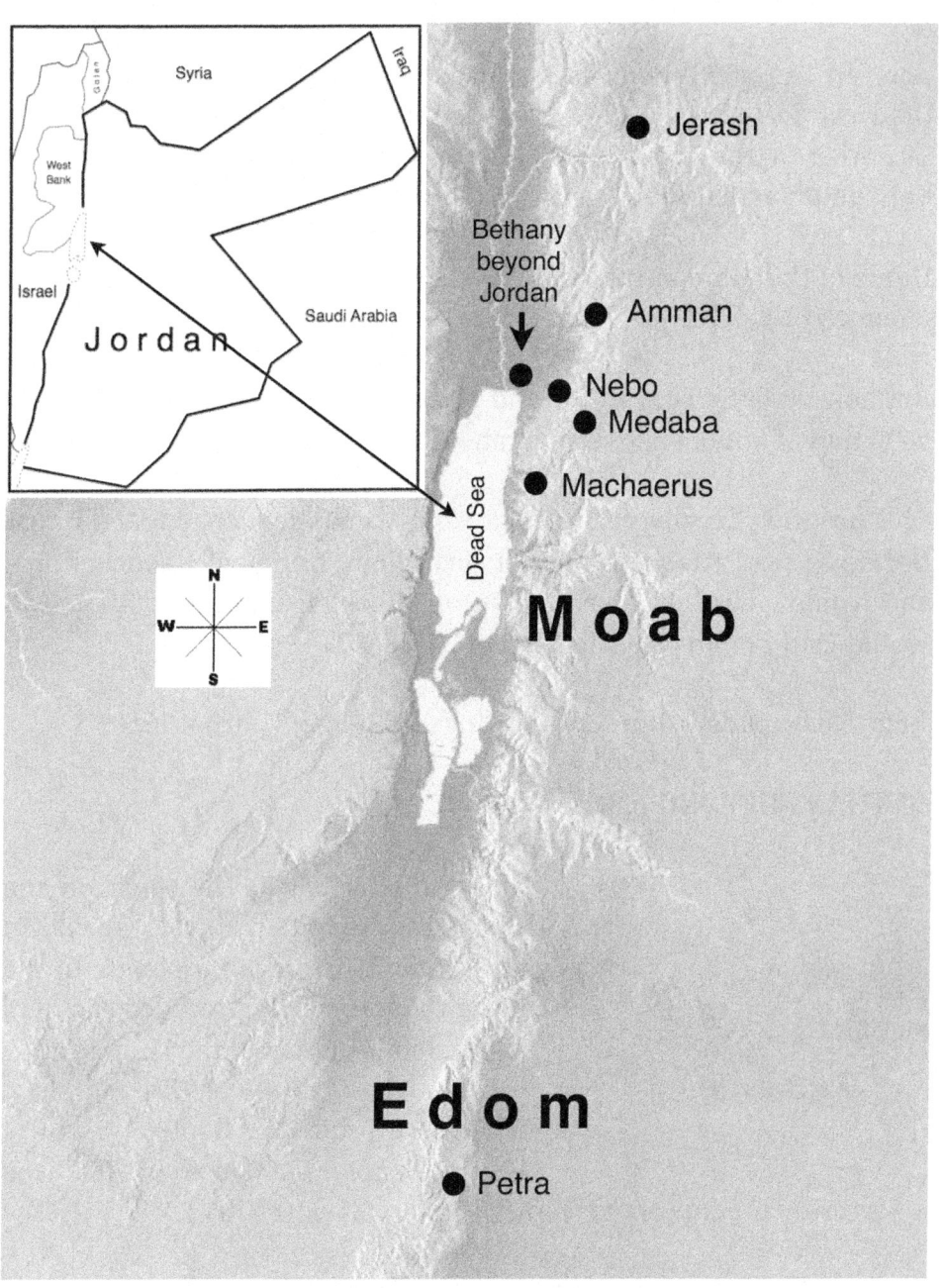

# Major Sites In Jordan

**AMMAN:** Rabbath-amman, Philadelphia - Ammonites

The Old Testament knows Amman as Rabbah or Rabbath-amman. By the New Testament times, it was known as Philadelphia, one of the 10 cities of the Decapolis. The Decapolis Philadelphia is not the Philadelphia mentioned in the letter of Revelation 3.

Home of the Ammonites, one of Israel's longstanding and formidable enemies - Nu. 21:23-24; Judg. 3:12-14; 2nd Sam. 10:1-19; Is. 11:14

Ammon was the son of Lot and one of his daughters after the destruction of Sodom and Gomorrah - Gen. 19:30-38.

The prophet Ezekiel recorded a time when Nebuchadnezzar must decide to first attack Amman or Jerusalem. Although Nebuchadnezzar would seek his own divination, Ezekiel announced that God would lead him to Jerusalem - Eze. 21:18-27.

References: Judg. 10:6-12:3; 1st Kings 11:1-5; 2nd Chron. 12:13

## BETHANY BEYOND JORDAN

This Bethany is not the town on the east side of the Mt. of Olives in Jerusalem. It is on the east side of the Jordan River, not far from Jericho, and about 3 miles north of the Dead Sea.

It's where John (the Baptizer) said of Jesus, *"Behold the Lamb of God who takes away the sins of the world!"* - John 1:28-29 (NKJV).

Later, Jesus would return to the area and many would believe in Him - John 10:40-42.

While the Bible only mentions that Elijah "crossed over" the Jordan River" this is a traditional site of his ascension into heaven in a "fiery chariot" - 2nd Kings 2:1-11.

## EDOM - Edomites

Edomites were the descendents of Esau - Gen. 25:24-25 compare 25:30.

The clan settled in the area of Seir (also called Mt. Seir). Seir is located between the Dead Sea and the Red Sea. Petra is a famous site in that region. - Gen. 36:1, 8.

The book of Obadiah announced God's judgment against the Edomites.

References: Gen. 20:14-22; 2nd Sam. 8:13-14; 1st Kings 19:26; Psa. 137: 7

## JERASH: Gerasa

The biblical city of Gerasa is known today as Jerash. Gerasa was one of the cities of the Roman Decapolis and is one of the best preserved cities of the Decapolis. Jerash is about 25 miles north of Amman.

Jesus went with His disciples to Gerasa - Luke 8:26 "Then they sailed to the country of the Gerasenes [that is, people from Gerasa], which is opposite Galilee."

## KING'S HIGHWAY

This north/south road is mentioned by name in the Bible (Nu. 20:17 and 21:22). It's called the King's Highway and it was the route that

Moses wished to follow as he led his people north through the land of Edom, which is in southern Jordan.

The name, however, may have come from an earlier episode recorded in Genesis 14. An alliance of "4 kings from the north" marched their troops along this route to do battle against the "5 kings of the Cities of the Plain," including the wicked cities of Sodom and Gomorrah. The invading monarchs captured Lot, Abraham's nephew before retreating. Abraham chased down the king and overpowered them near Damascus and rescued his nephew.

## MACHAERUS

Located about 15 miles southwest of the modern-day Medaba, Machaerus was the hilltop fortress of Herod the Great.

Thought to be the location where John (the Baptizer) was beheaded after condemning Herod Antipas for divorcing his wife to marry his sister-in-law, Herodias - Mt. 14:1-2; Mark 6:14-29.

The Machaerus fortress is similar to the Herodion, another hilltop fortress near Bethlehem (see pp. 83- 84). It is situated in the mountains on the east side of the Dead Sea on the top of a conical hill about 3,800 feet above the Dead Sea.

**MEDABA**: Madaba, Madeba

Medaba is famous for a floor mosaic in the St. George Greek Orthodox church. It is the oldest surviving cartographic depiction of the Holy Land known today. Originally it measured roughly 65 X 23 ft. What remains today is about 50 X 15 ft.

The map covers a geographical area from Lebanon to the Nile Delta (N/S), and from the Mediterranean Sea to the Eastern Desert (W/E).

Central in this mosaic is a depiction of Byzantine Jerusalem.

The Israelites defeated Sihon, king of the Amorites, and destroyed Medaba - Nu. 21:30.

Medaba was part of the land inheritance of Reuben - Josh. 13:9, 16.

Armies camps at Medaba to fight against David - 1st Chron. 19:7.

**MOAB** - Moabites

The land of Moab extended south and east from the southern edge of the Dead Sea. At its peak of power, it extended beyond the north edge of the Dead Sea. When Moses died, he was buried in the "land of Moab," while the people mourned his death 30 days in the "plains of Moab." (Deut. 34:5, 8)

Moab was the son of Lot and one of his daughters after the destruction of Sodom and Gomorrah - Gen. 19:30-38.

Balak, king of Moab, sought a famous diviner, Balaam, to pronounce a curse on Israel. Balaam could not do it. Instead, he suggested that the king entice the Israelites with the pleasures of Moab, saying that God would pronounce His own judgment against them for participating in it - Num. 22-25.

Ruth was a Moabitess - Ruth 1:1-5.

References: 2nd Kings 3; Isaiah 11:14; Isaiah 15-16; Jer. 48; Neh. 13:23-27

**MT. NEBO**

Mt. Nebo is about 3,000 ft in elevation and is the place from where Moses saw the Promised Land, but was not allowed to enter it. It is located about 15 miles east of Jericho at the northern tip of the Dead Sea.

It is closely associated with Mt. Pisgah - compare Deut. 32:49; 34:1.

**PETRA**

Archaeologists believe that Petra is over 7000 years old, putting it in the same category with Jericho as one of the earliest known settlements in the Middle East. Petra is in the land of Edom. (See EDOM, p. 131)

The Bible tells of how King David subdued the Edomites, approximately 1000 B.C. According to this account, the Edomites were enslaved, but eventually won their freedom. A series of great battles were then fought between the Judeans and the people of Edom. In one of these the Judean King, Amaziah (796-781 B.C.), "defeated ten thousand Edomites in the Valley of Salt, and captured Sela in battle" - 2$^{nd}$ Kings 14:7.

Sela became better known by its Greek name, Petra. The summit of the Umm al-Biyara mountain in central Petra is often identified as the Sela of the Bible. It should be pointed out, however, that Sela is also sometimes identified as the mountaintop stronghold of Sele, near Buseirah, one of the Edomite capitals north of Petra.

In 2007, Petra was introduced as one of the *New Seven Wonders of the Ancient World*. There are many ways to enter Petra, none of which are easy. The main entrance is called the Siq, a natural crack in the mountain with sides as high as 650 ft.

At the end of the Siq, you are captivated by the Treasury (Kazneh), popularized in the movie *Indiana Jones and the Last Crusade*.

The following map shows the general layout of what you will see on your visit to Petra.

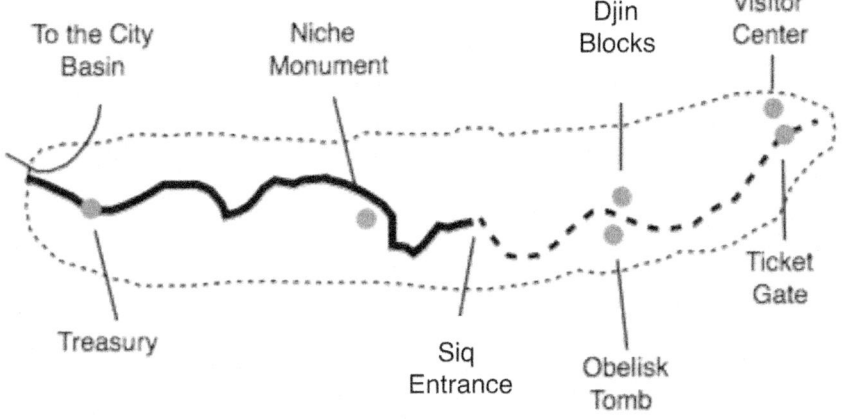

This photo shows an area in the "city basin." Roman influence is seen in the pillar-lined cobblestone road.

# Jordan Notes

# Jordan Notes

# Jordan Notes

# Jordan Notes

# Jordan Notes

# Egypt Supplement

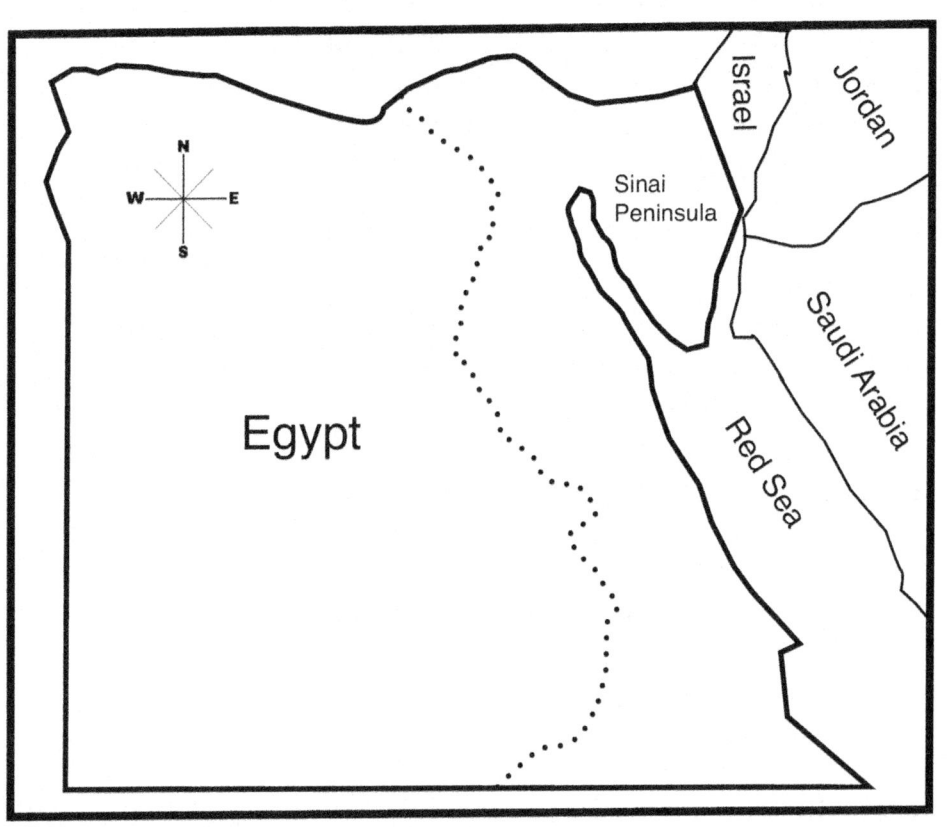

(see p. 54)

# A Brief History of Egypt through the Time of Solomon

(Adapted from my course on Old Testament History at West Coast Bible College and various websites, confirming and updating the material)

Egypt's history is long and glorious. Some of it is recorded for us in the biblical text, yet there remain many questions as to how its past relates to Bible history. Here's just one example. It is difficult to account for the Pharaohs in the Exodus story. Imminent scholars put it early (c. 1445 B.C.) in the reign of Amenhotep II. Others place it much later in history (c. 1240 B.C.) in the reign of Rameses II. There are reasonable arguments for each position, which confuses the non-scholarly who struggle to align biblical and secular history.

The following is a list of Old Testament events as they relate to Egypt. Please remember, this is a "broad stroke" of history not without controversy. The times given for these events so long ago should only be regarded as approximate dates. They are not intended to be non-negotiable, ironclad times.

**Middle Kingdom Period**: (Dynasty XI-XII, 2119-1800 B.C.)

- Abraham went to Egypt during this period
- Joseph was sold into slavery c. 1895 B.C.
- Joseph went before Pharaoh c. 1885 B.C.
- Israel moved to Egypt c. 1875 B.C.
- Joseph died c. 1800 B.C.

**Second Intermediate Period**: (Dynasties XIII-XVII, 1800-1570 B.C.)

- The Hyksos came to rule in the 13th Dynasty c. 1800 B.C. During this time, the Israelites probably lived in a peaceful relationship with their Semite brothers.

**Eighteenth (XVIII) Dynasty** (1570-1304 B.C.)

- Ahmose I ended the Hyksos rule c. 1570 B.C. He is likely the

Pharaoh mentioned *"who did not know about Joseph"* - Ex. 1:8 (NIV).

- Amenhotep I was the son of Ahmose I. He or his father could be the pharaoh who oppressed the Israelites - Ex. 1:11-14. He died c. 1525 B.C.

- Thutmose I began his reign c. 1525 B.C. He is likely the king who instructed the midwives to kill the male sons born to the Hebrew women - Ex. 1:15. He was the first Pharoah to be buried in the Valley of the Kings.

- Moses was born c. 1525 B.C. That would have been right at the beginning of the reign of Thutmose I. If that is the case, then his daughter, Hatshepsut, would be "the daughter of Pharaoh" who found Moses in the "bulrush" - Ex. 2:1-10.

- By the time Moses was 40 years of age, c. 1485 B.C., Hatshepsut had married both Thutmose II and III. Tutmose III was very young when his father died, so she reigned with him as co-regent. She gained so much control and power that he would not be able to rule as king until after her death. Moses killed an Egyptian during their joint rule. Remember, Moses had been found and raised by Hatshepsut, which made him a possible heir to the throne of Egypt. By eliminating Moses, he not only eliminated a rival to the throne, but also attempted to regain some of the authority lost to his wife/Mother, Hatshepsut. *"When Pharaoh heard of this, he tried to kill Moses"* - Ex. 2:15 (NIV).

- Thutmose III died c. 1450 B.C. Moses would have been 75 years old. The death of Thutmose III may have prompted the "burning bush" experience as God heard the cries of His people - Ex. 2:23-24.

- Amenhotep II, the son of Thutmose III, was the next to rule. If the Exodus happened early, c. 1445 B.C., then he was the Pharaoh during the Exodus.

- Thutmose IV, son of Amenhotep II, was next to the throne. He would have been the Pharaoh while the Children of Israel wandered in the wilderness.

- Amenhotep III, next to the throne, would have been the Pharoah when the Children of Israel entered the Promised Land. His reign, for the most part was prosperous and peaceful. He had the sixty ft tall statues of himself to be made. They are known as *the Colossi of Memnon.*

**Nineteenth (XIX) Dynasty** (1292-1185 B.C.)

- Rameses II, c. 1279-1213 B.C., was the third Pharaoh in the Nineteenth Dynasty, following Rameses I and Seti I, another of Rameses I's sons. For those who follow a late Exodus, c. 1240 B.C., he is the Pharaoh of the Exodus.

**Twenty first (XXI) Dynasty** (1069-945 B.C.)

- During the reigns of David and Solomon, Israel did not come under attack by the Egyptians. One could easily explain peace during Solomon's reign because he married Pharaoh's daughter - 1st Kings 3:1.

(One more notation, which happened after Solomon's reign):

**Twenty second (XXII) Dynasty** (945-736 B.C.)

- Sheshonq/Shishak came to the throne in 945 B.C. Fifteen years later, he invaded Jerusalem during the reign of Rehoboam and took away Temple treasures - 1st Kings 14:25-28.

# Mummy Dearest

The mummification process practiced in ancient Egypt fascinates many people. At the time of death, the person to be mummified was taken to the tent known as ibu or "place of purification". There the embalmers washed the body with a sweet smelling palm wine and rinse it with water from the Nile. After the initial cleansing, the body was then taken to the embalmer's house for the actual mummification process.

All the vital organs were removed because they are the first part of the body to decompose. The liver, lungs, stomach, and intestines were removed, washed in natron (to dry them out), and placed in canopic jars. The lids of these jars were often decorated with images representing the four sons of Horus. NOTE: The heart was not removed because it was thought to be the center of intelligence and feeling; the person in the afterlife would need it.

After forty days the embalmers again washed the body with water from the Nile, repacked the body with clean natron, and wrapped it in linen wrappings soaked in resin and aromatic oils. The resin and oils were to help the skin stay elastic.

The head and neck were wrapped first. Strips of fine linen were used. Then the fingers and toes were wrapped individually. The arms and legs were wrapped separately. Between the layers of wrapping, the embalmers placed amulets, a small trinket or charm, that were meant to protect the person from evil spells or actions.

While the embalmers did their work, a priest would be called in to read spells out loud. These spells were intended to ward off evil spirits and help the deceased make his/her journey to the afterlife.

The arms and legs were then tied together. Usually a papyrus scroll with spells from the *Book of the Dead* was placed between the wrapped hands.

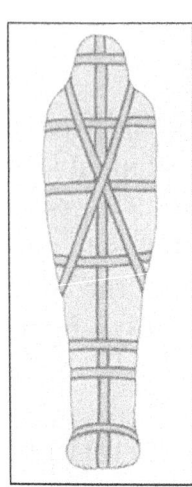
More strips of linen were wrapped around the body. At every layer, the strips were painted with liquid resin to help 'glue' the bandages together. Sometimes, a picture of the god Osiris was painted on its surface.

Finally, a large cloth was wrapped around the entire mummy. It was secured with strips of linen horizontally, vertically, and diagonally.

A board of painted wood was placed on top of the mummy before it was lowered into a coffin. The first coffin was then put into a second coffin.

The entire process from death to burial took about seventy days. The mummification portion took forty days, and it took an additional fifteen days to wrap the body. During that time the tomb was prepared with everything the deceased would need in the afterlife.

If the person was rich, the coffins were placed inside a stone sarcophagus, in a tomb. Furniture, clothing, valuable objects, food and drink were arranged in the tomb for the deceased.

In the case of a king or potentate, slaves were also put in the tomb to assist their masters in the afterlife.

Interestingly, the patriarchs Jacob and Joseph were mummified following Egyptian procedures.

*When Jacob had finished giving instructions to his sons, he drew his feet up into the bed, breathed his last and was gathered to his people. Joseph threw himself upon his father and wept over him and kissed him. Then Joseph directed the physicians in his service to embalm his father Israel. So the physicians embalmed him, taking a full forty days, for that was the time required for embalming. And the Egyptians mourned for him seventy days.* (Gen. 49:33-50:3 NIV)

*So Joseph died at the age of a hundred and ten. And after they embalmed him, he was placed in a coffin in Egypt.* (Gen. 50:26 NIV)

# The Gods of Egypt

As God prepared His people to leave Egypt at the time of the Exodus, He vowed to bring judgment against their gods. Two Scripture passages that announce this are Exodus 12:12 and Numbers 33:4. God said that He would *"go through the land of Egypt"* to *"strike down all the firstborn in the land."* One reason for this decisive judgment was to bring about God's judgment *"against all the gods of Egypt."* This dramatic demonstration of His power would prove that He alone was God.

The Egyptians worshiped a pantheon of at least sixty gods and goddesses. Among them you will find the following:

**Amun Re** or **Amun Ra**; the chief god of the New Kingdom, considered to be the king of the gods. Represented by a man with a crown of (falcon) feathers.

**Anubis**; a very ancient god of death and the netherworld. Represented by a man with the head of a dog or jackal.

**Apis**; ancient bull god associated with the city of Memphis and chief of the cult of the sacred bulls. Represented by a bull.

**Aten**; the chief deity adopted by Amenhotep IV / Akhenaton c. 1372-1353 B.C. Represented by a solar disk with rays reaching earth.

**Bes**; god of children and protector in childbirth. Represented by a dwarf.

**Heqet**; goddess of childbirth and fertility. Represented by a woman with a frog's head.

**Horakhte/Harakhty**; an early national god aka "Horus of the two horizons" (sunrise and sunset). Represented by a man with the head of a falcon on which is a solar disk.

**Horus**; the earliest and most significant of the national gods of Egypt. The pharaoh was believed to be the incarnation of Horus. Represented by a man with the head of a falcon.

**Isis**; a goddess and wife of Osiris (some believe her to be the mother of Horus). She was the goddess of motherhood and children, as well as the patron of nature and magic. Represented by a woman with a headdress shaped like a throne.

**Khepri**; god of the emerging sun (sunrise), overseeing the cycle of life and death. Represented by a man with the head of a scrub beetle.

**Maat/Mayet**; the daughter of Re, and goddess of truth, justice, and cosmic order. Represented by a woman with an ostrich feather in her headband.

**Neith**; goddess of war and hunting. Represented by a woman with a headdress of crossed arrows and a shield.

**Nut**; the sky goddess. Represented by a star-covered human arching over the earth.

**Osiris**; god of vegetation and the afterlife. Represented by a man with green skin (vegetation), mummy-wrapped legs, a distinctive crown with ostrich feathers, and carrying a crook and flail (afterlife).

**Re/Ra**; early Egyptian god of the sun and creative power. Represented by a man with a falcon head upon which rests the sun.

**Set**; god of storms and chaos and the guardian of crops. Represented by a man with the head of an unknown animal (perhaps a horse or donkey).

**Sobek**; god of the Nile and the patron of armies and military. Represented by a man with the head of a crocodile.

**Thoth**; god of wisdom and science (knowledge/writing). Represented by a man with the head of an ibis or baboon.

**Wadket**; goddess of fire and heat. Represented by a cobra with a woman's head.

# Map of Major Sites in Egypt

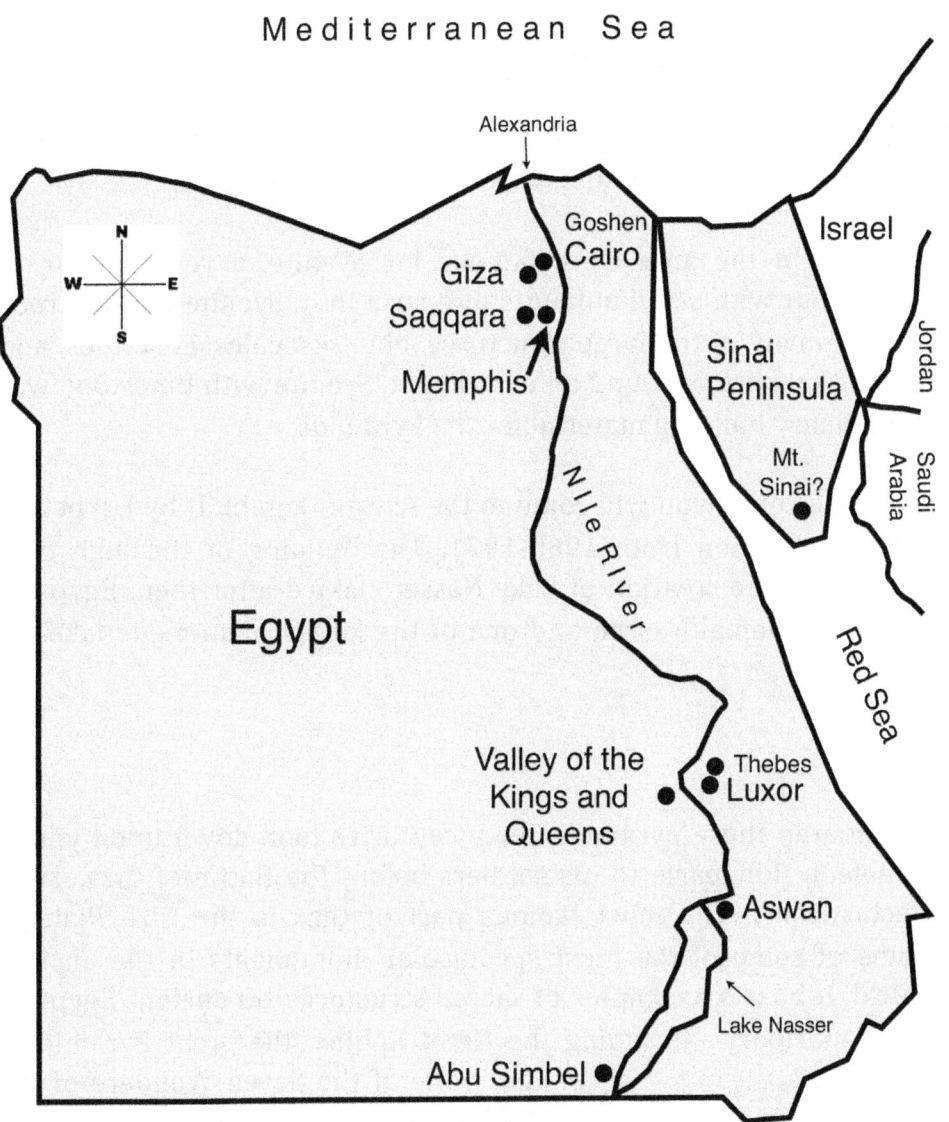

## Major Sites in Egypt

### ASWAN

Aswan is the ancient city of Swenet, which in antiquity was a frontier town in the south, and gateway to the main caravan route leading to Nubia (Sundan today) and all points south. Swenet may have derived its name from an Egyptian goddess with the same name.

Quarries in the area were famous for Syenite, a rock similar to granite but with small amounts of quartz in it. Syenite was the rock used in many of the large structures, obelisks, colossal statues, and monolithal shrines found all over Egypt. Syenite with limestone was the primary building material for the Pyramids.

Traveling south, you will come to the Aswan Dam built by Egypt and the Soviet Union from 1960-1971. The building of the high dam resulted in the creation of Lake Nasser, named after then, Egyptian President, Gamal Nasser, and one of the largest man-made lakes in the world.

### GIZA

"From atop these pyramids, forty centuries look down upon you" - Napoleon Bonaparte to his soldiers before the Battle of Giza, 1798 (factasy.com). The most famous part of Giza is the Giza Plateau, home of some of the most spectacular monuments in the ancient world. It boasts a complex of sacred structures, an ancient Egyptian royal mortuary—including the Great Sphinx, the great Pyramid of Giza (one of the Seven Wonders of the Ancient World)—and a number of other large pyramids and temples.

All three pyramids were built during the Third and Fourth Dynasties, resulting from monumental effort by the king and the royal sons following them.

The Pyramid of Cheops (Khufu), the largest of the pyramids, has a base that covers roughly a nine acre area (approximately 392,040 square feet) and stands 450 feet high. Herodotus, in his historical account, says it took 100,000 men, working in 3-month shifts, 20 years to build it. (Herodotus, *History 2.124-25*)

## GOSHEN

The "Land of Goshen" is an area more than a city. It was in the northeastern corner of Egypt near the Via Mares (International Highway), the main commercial route leading to Asia Minor and Mesopotamia.

After Joseph became a leader in Egypt, he asked Pharaoh's permission to set up his family in Goshen - Gen. 46:28-47:6.

A new Pharaoh came to power who feared that the Israelites might become a danger to his power. He forced them to build the storehouse cities of Pithom and Rameses - Ex. 1: 8-14.

There were both Israelites and Egyptians living in Goshen when God sent the plagues to Egypt. Some of the plagues affected the Egyptians only - Ex. 8:20-9:26.

## THEBES/KARNAK/LUXOR

The history of the Karnak complex is largely the history of Thebes. Thebes is merely the Greek name for the ancient Karnak located in the modern city of Luxor. The vast complex was built and enlarged over a period of thirteen hundred years and does not appear to have been of any significance before the Eleventh Dynasty.

Among the earliest artifacts found in the area of the temple mentions Amun-Re. Amun, sometimes called Amen, was long the local god of Thebes.

Thebes was destroyed by the Assyrians in 663 B.C. The prophet Nahum asked Niniveh if they thought themselves "better than Thebes" - Nahum 3:8.

The prophet Jeremiah said that God would bring "punishment upon Amon of Thebes." That punishment would come at the hand of the Babylonians - Jer. 46:25.

Some scholars think Moses spent part of his childhood in Thebes, at the house of Pharaoh. If this is so, he would have first hand knowledge of the "treasures of Egypt" that Hebrews says he ultimately rejected - Heb. 11:23-26.

## MEMPHIS

According to Herodotus, the city was founded c. 3100 B.C. by Menes. Its ancient name was Ineb Hedj—White Walls. The name "Memphis" is the Greek corruption of the Egyptian name of one of the pyramid complexes, which was called Mennefer or Menfe.

The prophet Hosea mentions Memphis in regards to its people burying Israelites there - Hosea 9:6.

Jeremiah warned the Jews living in Memphis that if they didn't change their evil ways, the same destruction at the hand of Nebuchadnezzar that befell Jerusalem would also be theirs - Jer. 44:1-14.

## MT. SINAI

Mt. Sinai is the name of a specific mountain as well as a range of mountains. No one knows the exact location of the Sinai mentioned in the Exodus story. Our guide told us that there are 24 mountain peaks claiming to be the original Sinai!

One such peak is Jebel Musa—the Mountain of Moses—located in the southern tip of the Sinai Peninsula. The peak of this 7,500 ft mountain is reached by climbing over 3,700 steps, carved out by monks from St. Catherine's Monastery at its base. There is a chapel on the summit, built atop an ancient chapel built c. 365 A.D.

The original monastery at the base of Mt. Sinai was constructed by Justinian c. 565 A.D. It was built around the traditional location of Moses and the burning bush.

**SAQQARA**: Sakkara

Sakkara is a vast, ancient burial ground in Egypt, featuring the world's oldest standing, step pyramid. While Memphis was the capital of ancient Egypt, Sakkara served as its necropolis. Although it was later eclipsed by the burial ground of royalty at Giza and still later by the Valley of the Kings in Thebes, it remained an important complex for minor burials and cult ceremonies for more than three millennia. Imhotep designed the step pyramid at Sakkara for King Dioser (c. 2667-2648 B.C.). It is the oldest complete hewn-stone building complex known in history. The tomb of the first pharaoh in Egypt, Menes, is in Sakkara.

**VALLEY OF THE KINGS AND QUEENS**

Starting with the 18th Dynasty c. 1570 (time of Moses) through the 20th Dynasty c. 1569 (time of David and Solomon), the Valley of the Kings and Queens became the necropolis of the pharaohs. Abandoning the Pyramid type tombs of Sakkara and Giza, they began to build massive monuments in caves along the Nile River.

The Valley of the Kings and Queens is located opposite Thebes/Luxor on the west side of the Nile. The Kings area has 63 tombs as of this writing, while the Queen section, just to the southwest, has 80 tombs. It isn't 100% accurate to call it is the burial site of the kings and queens. For example, only 25 of the 63 tombs in the kings area have been designated as royal tombs. Perhaps it would be better said, the burial site of nobility, which is vastly different than some descriptions of the area. According to Siliotti, the official name is *The Great and Majestic Necropolis of the Millions of Years of the Pharaoh, Life, Strength, Health in the West of Thebes.* Or, shortened to, *The Great Field.* (Alberto Siliotti 1997, *Guide to the Valley of the Kings*, pp. 12-13)

Among the many discoveries in the area was that of Queen Hatshepsut, most likely the daughter of Pharaoh who discovered the baby Moses among the reeds of the Nile. The photo is her tomb.

Another great discovery was King Tut's tomb, excavated by Howard Carter in 1922. With the immeasurable wealth uncovered that day, Carter's now famous words can be understood. When he drilled a hole in the plaster door to expose the tomb, Lord Carnarvon, the money-man behind the expedition, asked, "Can you see anything?" Carter replied, "Yes, wonderful things!"

# Egypt Notes

# Egypt Notes

# Egypt Notes

# Egypt Notes

# Egypt Notes

# Egypt Notes

# Section III: *Additional Reference Material*

## APPENDIX 1: Vocabulary

This section on words and vocabulary was adapted from the *Israel Passenger Information Kit,* Ya'lla Tours USA, Inc. No © was listed.

In both ancient and modern Israel, Hebrew was/is the main language. Arabic is the official second language. However, English is widely spoken. On most tours, you'll never have to worry about communication. The following is a list of common words and phrases, should you be interested in knowing some Hebrew.

**Months of the Jewish Calendar**

| | |
|---|---|
| Tishrei | Sept/Oct |
| Heshvan | Oct/Nov |
| Kislev | Nov/Dec |
| Tevet | Dec/Jan |
| Shevat | Jan/Feb |
| Adar | Feb/Mar |
| Nissan | Mar/Apr |
| Iyar | Apr/May |
| Sivan | May/June |
| Tammuz | June/July |
| Av | July/Aug |
| Elul | Aug/Sept |

**Jewish Days of the Week**

| | |
|---|---|
| Yom Rishon | Sunday |
| Yom Sheni | Monday |

Yom Shushi — Tuesday
Yom Revi'i — Wednesday
Yom Hamishi — Thursday
Yom Shishi — Friday
Yom Shabbath — Saturday

**Words and Phrases**

Yes - *Ken*
No - *Lo*
Please - *Bevaksha*
Thank you - *Tada*
Excuse me - *Slicha*
Good morning - *Boker Tov*
Good evening - *Erev Tov*
Welcome - *Bruchim Habahim*
Good bye - *Shalom*
My name is ____ - *Korim li* ____
What is your name? - *Ma shimcha*
How are you? - *Ma shlomcha*
I speak English - *Ani medaber anglit*
Do you speak English? - *Haim ata medaber anglit?*
Can you help me? - *Ata yachol li?*
Where is the bathroom? *Ehfo hah sherooteem?*
Restaurant - *Misada*
Breakfast - *Aruchat boker*
Lunch - *Aruchat zaharaim*
Dinner - *Aruchat erev*
Water - *Maim*
Mineral water - *Maim mineralim*
Wine - *Yain*

Glass - *Kos*
Plate - *Tzalachat*
Bread - *Lechem* (Bethlehem - House of BREAD)
Butter - *Chemha*
Olives - *Zeitim*
Cheese - *Gvina*
Salad - *Salat*
Vegetables - *Yerakot*
Meat - *Basar*
Chicken - *Of*
Fish - *Dag*
Dessert - *Liftan*
Fruit - *Pri*
Coffee - *Kafe*
Tea - Tei
Sugar - *Sucar*
Milk - *Chalav*
Hot - *Cham*
Cold - *Kar*
May I have the bill please? *Cheshbon bebakasha?*
Police - *Mishtara*
Hospital - *Beth Cholim*
Pharmacy - *Beth merkachat*
Doctor - *Rofe*
Please call a doctor. - *Bevakash tikra la rophe*
Money - *Kesef*
I would like to change some money. - *Ani Rotyze lehachlif kesef*
Change (coins) - *Matbeot*
Do you have any change? - *Yesh lecha odef?*
Price - *Mechir*

Where can I buy____? - *Eifo ani yachol liknot ____?*
How much is it? - *Cama?*
Shop/Store - *Chanut*
Newspaper - *Iton*
Book - *Sefer*

# APPENDIX 2: Hebrew Prayers

This section on prayers was adapted from the *JCF Biblical Study Tours: Introduction to the Land, Language and Literature of the Bible*. This study guide was produced for my 'From Dan to Beersheba' Tour of Israel w/Petra, 2012. © JCF Biblical Study Tours. JFC is Jerusalem Cornerstone Foundation, used with permission.

Morning prayer: Blessing before the Shema

*With an abundant love You have loved us, Lord our God; with exceedingly great pity have You pitied us.*

*Our Father, our King, for the sake of our forefathers who trusted in You and whom You taught the decrees of life, may You be equally gracious to us and teach us.*

*Our Father, the merciful Father, Who acts mercifully, have mercy upon us; instill in our hearts to understand and elucidate, to listen, learn, teach, safeguard, perform, and fulfill all the words of Your Torah's teaching with love.*

*Enlighten our eyes in Your Torah, attach our hearts to Your commandments, and unify our hearts to love and fear Your name.*

**The Shema:**

*Hear Oh Israel, the Lord is our God, the Lord is one! Blessed is the Name of His glorious kingdom forever and ever.*

*You shall love the Lord your God with all of your heart, with all your soul and with all your strength. And these words, which I command you today shall be in your heart. You shall teach them diligently to your children, and shall talk of them when you sit in your house, when you walk by the way, when you lie down, and when you rise up. You shall bind them as a sign on your hand, and they shall be as frontlets between your eyes. You shall write them on the doorposts of your house and on your gates.*

*And you shall love your neighbor as yourself.*

**The Kaddish**: The sanctification of God's Name

This prayer is associated with loss. For example, an observant Jew will mourn the death of a loved one for seven days. For the next eleven months he is still considered a mourner. During that time he will lead this community prayer in the synagogue.

It honors God's name, which is difficult to do in times of grief. It is not intended to be prayed privately, but rather publicly. The words of this prayer draw the focus away from himself to God, who even in the midst of sorrow can heal the broken heart.

*Glorified and sanctified be God's great name throughout the world which He has created according to His will.*

*May He establish His kingdom in your lifetime and during your days, and within the life of the entire House of Israel, speedily and soon; and say, Amen.*

*May His great name be blessed forever and to all eternity.*

*Blessed and praised, glorified and exalted, extolled and honored, adored and lauded be the name of the Holy One, blessed be He, beyond all the blessings and hymns, praises and consolations that are ever spoken in the world; and say, Amen.*

*May there be abundant peace from heaven, and life, for us and for all Israel; and say Amen.*

*He who creates peace in heaven, may He create peace for us and for all Israel; and say, Amen.*

# The Amidah (Standing Prayer): 19 Blessings

The Amidah is prayed silently during the synagogue service. It is a time where each person is to stand personally before God; to praise Him, and to intercede as an individual.

1. God of History: *O Lord, open my lips, and my mouth shall declare Your praise. Blessed art Thou, O Lord our God and God of our fathers; God of Abraham, God of Isaac, and God of Jacob, the great, mighty, and revered God, the most high God, Who bestows loving kindness, and the Master of all things; Who remembers the pious deeds of the patriarchs, and in love will bring a Redeemer to their children's children for Your name's sake.*

2. God of Nature: *O King, Helper, Savior, and Shield. Blessed art You, O Lord, the Shield of Abraham, You, O Lord, are mighty forever, You revive the dead, You are mighty to save. You sustain the living with loving kindness, revive the dead with great mercy, support the failing, heal the sick, free the bound, and keep Your faith to them that sleep in the dust. Who is like You, Lord of mighty acts, and who resembles You, O King, Who orders death and restores life, and causes salvation to spring forth? Yes, You are faithful to revive the dead. Blessed art You, O Lord, Who revives the dead.*

3. God who sanctifies: *We will sanctify Your name in the world even as they sanctify it in the highest heavens, as it is written by the hand of Your prophet: "And they call to one another and said, holy, holy, holy, is the Lord of Hosts: the whole earth is full of His glory. Blessed be the glory of the Lord from His place." And in Your holy words it is written, saying: "The Lord shall reign forever, You are God, O Zion, unto all generations. Praise ye the Lord. Unto all generations we will declare Your greatness, and to all eternity we will proclaim Your holiness, and Your praise. O our God, You shall not depart from our mouth forever, for You are a great and holy God and King. Blessed art You, O Lord the holy God.*

4. Prayer for understanding: *You favor man with knowledge, and teach mortals understanding. Favor us with knowledge, understanding and discernment from You. Blessed are You, O Lord, gracious Giver of knowledge.*

5. Prayer for repentance: *Cause us to return, our Father, unto Your Torah; draw us near, our King, unto Your service, and bring us back in perfect repentance unto Your presence. Blessed art You, O Lord, who delights in repentance.*

6. Prayer for forgiveness: *Forgive us, our Father, for we have sinned; pardon us, our King, for we have transgressed; for You do pardon and forgive. Blessed art You, O Lord, who is gracious, and does abundantly forgive.*

7. Prayer for deliverance from affliction: *Look upon our affliction and plead our cause, and redeem us speedily for Your name's sake; for You are a mighty Redeemer. Blessed are You, O Lord, the Redeemer of Israel. (On days of fasting, include: Answer us, O Lord, answer us on this day of the fast of our humiliation, for we are in great trouble. Turn not to our wickedness; do not hide Your face from us nor hide Yourself from our supplication. Be near, we beseech You, unto our cry; let Your loving kindness be a comfort to us; even before we call unto You answer us, as it is written, " And it shall come to pass that, before they call, I will answer; while they are yet speaking, I will hear." For you, O Lord, are He Who answers in time of trouble, who delivers and rescues in all times of trouble and distress; the holy King.)*

8. Prayer for healing: *Heal us, O Lord, and we shall be healed; save us and we shall be saved; for You are our praise. Grant a perfect healing to all our wounds; for You, almighty King, are a faithful and merciful Physician. Blessed are You O Lord, who heals the sick of Your people Israel.*

9. Prayer for deliverance from want: *Bless this year unto us, O Lord our God, together with every kind of the produce for our welfare; give*

*a blessing upon the face of the earth. Satisfy us with Your goodness, and bless our year like other good years. Blessed are You, O Lord, who blesses the years.*

10. Prayer for reunion of Israel: *Sound the great horn for our freedom; raise the ensign to gather our exiles, and gather us from the four corners of the earth. Blessed are You, O Lord, who gathers the dispersed of Your people Israel.*

11. Prayer for the righteous reign of God: *Restore our judges as in former times, and our counselors as at the beginning; remove from us sorrow and sighing. Reign over us, O Lord. You alone, in loving kindness and tender mercy clear us in judgment. Blessed are You, O Lord, the King who loves righteousness and judgment.*

12. Prayer against slanderers: *And for slanderers let there be no hope, and let all wickedness perish as in a moment; let all Your enemies be speedily cut off, and the dominion of arrogance uproot and crush, cast down and humble speedily in our days. Blessed are You, O Lord, who breaks the enemies and humbles the arrogant.*

13. Prayer for the righteous and converts: *Toward the righteous and the pious, toward the elders of Your people the house of Israel, toward the remnant of their scribes, toward true converts, and toward us also may Your tender mercies be stirred, O Lord our God. Grant a good reward to all who faithfully trust in Your name. Set our portion with them forever, so that we may not be put to shame, for we have trusted in You. Blessed are You, O Lord the stay and trust of the righteous.*

14. Prayer for the rebuilding of Jerusalem: *And Jerusalem, Your city, return in mercy, and dwell therein as You have spoken. Rebuild it soon in our days as an everlasting building, and speedily set up therein the throne of David. Blessed are You, O Lord, Who rebuilds Jerusalem.*

15. Prayer for the Messianic King: *Speedily cause the offspring of David, Your servant, to flourish, and lift up His glory by Your divine*

*help because we wait for Your salvation all the day. Blessed are You, O Lord, Who causes the strength of salvation to flourish.*

16. Prayer for the hearing of prayer: *Hear our voice, O Lord our God; spare us and have mercy upon us, and accept our prayer in mercy and favor; for You are a "God Who hears and answers prayers and supplications." From Your presence, O our King, turn us not away empty. For You hear and answer in mercy the prayers of Your people Israel. Blessed are You, O Lord, Who hears and answers prayer.*

17. Prayer for the restoration of Temple service: *Accept, O Lord our God, Your people Israel and their prayer. Restore the service to the inner sanctuary of Your house. Receive in love and favor both the offerings of Israel and their prayer, and may the worship of Your people Israel be ever acceptable unto You. And let our eyes behold Your return in mercy to Zion. Blessed are You, O Lord, Who restores Your divine presence to Zion.*

18. Thanksgiving for God's unfailing mercies (spoken out loud by the leader of the Prayer Service): *We give thanks to You for You are the Lord our God and God of our Fathers for ever and ever. You are the Rock of our lives, the Shield of our salvation through every generation. We will give thanks to You and declare Your praise for our lives, which are committed into Your hand, and for our souls, which are in Your charge, and for Your miracles, which are daily with us, and for Your wonders and Your benefits, which are wrought at all times, evening, morning, and noon. You are all good, whose mercies fail not. You are the merciful One, whose loving kindness never ceases. We have ever hoped in You.*

(While the prayer leader says the paragraph above, the congregation recites the following in an undertone):

*We give thanks unto You for You are the Lord our God, and the God of our fathers, the God of all flesh, our Creator and the Creator of all things in the beginning. Blessings and thanksgiving be to Your great and holy Name, because You have kept us in life and have preserved us, so may You continue to keep us in life and preserve us. Gather our exiles to Your holy courts to observe Your statutes, to do Your will, and to serve You with a perfect heart. Blessed be the God to Whom thanksgiving is due.*

19. Grant Peace: *Grant peace, welfare, blessing, grace, loving kindness, and mercy unto us and unto all Israel, Your people. Bless us, O our Father, even all of us together, with the light of Your countenance. For by the light of Your countenance You have given us, O Lord our God, the Torah of life, loving kindness and righteousness, blessing, mercy, life and peace. May it be good in Your sight to bless Your people Israel at all times and in every hour with Your peace. Blessed are You, O Lord, who blesses Your people Israel with peace.*

# APPENDIX 3: Top Archaeological Discoveries of the 20th Century

Selecting the top archaeological discoveries is at the discretion of the one choosing the events. That is the case here. I have selected things that have significance for biblical understanding.

## THE DEAD SEA SCROLLS

The Dead Sea Scrolls were discovered in 1947, not by trained archaeologists, but by Bedouin shepherds. Pottery jars with scrolls and scroll fragments were discovered in a cave at Qumran, overlooking the Dead Sea.

Subsequent discoveries led to documents being found in eleven caves. Also excavated were the ruins of Khirbet Qumran. This happened while Israel was becoming a State (1948).

Among the documents were complete copies or portions of the entire Old Testament, with the exception of Esther. These scrolls were 1,000 years older than the previous texts at our disposal.

Other documents found there reveal the environment into which Christianity developed in Israel. There were no New Testament texts found, however many documents tell us a lot about the time leading up to the 1st Jewish revolt

The Dead Sea Scrolls are mainly housed in the Shrine of the Book, part of the Israel Museum in Jerusalem. The Copper Scroll is housed the Archaeological Museum in Amman, Jordan. Other small fragments reside in the Rockefeller Museum also in Jerusalem.

## THE HOUSE OF DAVID INSCRIPTION

This important discovery was made at Tel Dan (near Caesarea Philippi - Banias) at the foot of Mt. Hermon. In 1993 a broken fragment of basalt stone was uncovered. Upon careful examination, an inscription was discovered on the stone.

The inscription mentions King David's dynasty as, 'the House of David'. It is the first mention of 'the House of David' outside of the biblical record. Pottery fragments and other items at the site date the stone at the end of the 9th or beginning of the 8th century B.C.

## AMULET SCROLL

1979 gave us another important archaeological discovery. In a burial cave on the southwestern slope of the Hinnom Valley (next to the Scottish Presbyterian Church of St. Andrew) a repository of grave goods was found. Among the approximately 700 items unearthed was a silver, rolled amulet. Inscribed on it were the letters of the Tetragrammaton, the name of God, YHWH.

The date of the tomb was set as the late seventh to early sixth century B.C., the end of the Davidic dynasty. This discovery gives us the oldest extra-Biblical evidence for the name of God recovered in Jerusalem. A scripture passage on the amulet is from the Aaronic (priestly) blessing found in Numbers 6:24-25.

## GALILEE BOAT

A severe drought in 1985-86 brought the Sea of Galilee to unusually low levels, exposing large areas of the lakebed along the shoreline. Two brothers discovered the remains of a boat buried in the mud along the shore. Israeli archaeologists were able to confirm that it was an ancient rather than a modern craft. Later it was determined to be 2,000 years old. This was the first time an ancient boat had been discovered at the Sea of Galilee.

It is on display at the Nof Ginosar Boat Museum at the Sea of Galilee. Carbon-14 testing put the date of the boat around 120-40 B.C.

It was estimated that the boat could accommodate four oarsmen, a helmsman, and a dozen individuals. It is similar to the boat Jesus and the disciples would have used.

## THE BARUCH BULLA

A bulla (or bullae) is a seal impression of clay. Think of an official document that was folded or rolled up. It would be tied with string and a dollop of soft clay would be put on the knot of the string. The surface of the clay would then be impressed with a signet ring, thus identifying the owner.

Normally the clay is fragile and over time, easily destroyed. During the 1970's, a bulla with the name of Jeremiah's scribe, Baruch, was found. It had survived, in part, because the area where it was found had encountered a fire. The heat acted as a kiln of sorts, and fired the clay seal.

The inscription on the bulla identified it as "Belonging to Baruch ben Neriah" the scribe who wrote for Jeremiah (36:4).

Also found was a seal bearing the inscription "Belonging to Seriah (ben) Neriah." Seriah was the "chief chamberlain" in the court of King Zedekiah (Jer. 51:59). Seriah ben Neriah was the brother of Baruch ben Neriah, and both were close friends of the prophet Jeremiah.

## OSSUARY OF CAIAPHAS

A dump truck accidentally smashed through the roof of a tomb in November 1990 during some work in the Jerusalem Peace Forest, leading to the discovery of the ossuary, which contained the bones of the High Priest in the time of Jesus.

An ossuary is a stone bone box, used for secondary burials. Initially the body is laid to rest in a burial niche. After decomposition, the bones were collected and placed in an ossuary, making the burial niche available for a subsequent burial. The most intricately carved ossuary was decorated with two circles each containing five rosettes, and twice carved into an undecorated side appears the name, "Yehosef bar Qafa'" (Joseph son of Caiaphas). The ossuary contained the remains of six people: two infants, a child aged 2 to 5, a boy aged 13 to 18, an adult female and a man about 60 years old. The latter are believed to be the bones of Caiaphas, before whom Jesus was brought for questioning.

## PONTIUS PILATE INSCRIPTION

Pontius Pilate was the fifth governor of Roman Judea, under whose governance Jesus was crucified. He was appointed by the emperor Tiberius in A.D. 26 and suspended by Vitellius, Roman governor of Syria, in A.D. 37, after slaughtering a number of Samaritans at Mt. Gerizim.

During excavations at Caesarea in 1961, a dedicatory stone was found that included the names of Tiberias, the Roman emperor at the time, and Pilate, called the prefect of Judea. The inscription not only confirms the historicity of Pilate, it clarifies the title that he bore as governor.

The stone is now on display in the Israel Museum in Jerusalem.

# APPENDIX 4: Biographical Sketches of Historical Figures, Groups, and Things

## Aelia Capitolina

In the aftermath of Rome's war against the Jews in 70 A.D., the Romans laid waste to the Second Temple—a devastating loss for the Jewish people. They also destroyed Herod's magnificent palace and the mansions of the upper city. Jerusalem lay in ruins, and Judea became nothing more than a province of Rome.

Ironically, when Emperor Hadrian vowed to rebuild Jerusalem from the wreckage in 130 A.D., it appeared he meant it as a gift to the Jewish people. But the building had to be on his terms, and therein lay the problem. Hadrian planned to build temples to pagan gods in the Holy City. And worst of all, he planned a temple to Jupiter on the Temple Mount where Solomon's Temple had once stood. That plan together with Hadrian's edicts against the practice of Judaism inflamed the Jews, who staged a massive, yet doomed revolt led by the warrior Bar Kochba.

Once the revolt had been crushed, Hadrian was free to resume his building project. But this time, the city of Jerusalem would not be for the Jews. To punish them, Hadrian exiled all Jews from Jerusalem, and imported residents from elsewhere in the world. Jerusalem became Aelia Capitolina—and for centuries, that was the only name that most people could remember. He even changed the name of the province from Judea to Palestine, a name meaning *Land of the Philistines,* perhaps intended to insult the Jews with the name of their long-standing enemy, Philistia.

Jerusalem was no longer the center of Judaism. The spiritual heart moved to the Galilee, where the most acclaimed Jewish leaders began to formulate the Talmud.

## Alexander the Great

Son of Philip II of Macedon, Alexander was born in 356 B.C. and died in 323 B.C. at the age of 32. He was tutored by Aristotle until he was 16 years old and by the age 30 he had created one of the largest empires of the ancient world. Many cities were named after him, most notably, Alexandria, Egypt.

Alexander introduced the Greek culture everywhere he conquered: Greek literature, myth, dance, language, money, medicine, art, and theater. Koine (common i.e. everyday) Greek became the lingua franca throughout the civilized world.

## Annas

His name means "the grace of Jehovah." He was the son of Seth and appointed high priest in 6 A.D. at age 37. He was high priest from 6 to 15 A.D. but as long as he lived, he was the virtual head of the priestly party in Jerusalem.

In the time of Christ, high priests were appointed and removed at the command of the Roman governors. Although removed from office, Annas' power and influence was so great that five of his sons, as well as his son-in-law Caiaphas and his grandson Matthias also became high priests. Even years after he lost the high priesthood, he was popularly considered as still in office and was called "high priest"; even after Pentecost his name appears first in the list of priestly leaders. (Acts 4:5-7)

Annas is referred to in connection with the beginning of John the Baptist's ministry, which took place "in the high-priesthood of Annas and Caiaphas" (Luke 3:2), as though father and son-in-law were joint holders of the office.

When Jesus was arrested, He was first brought before Annas. (John 18:13) It was apparently Annas who questioned Him about His disciples and His teaching, and who gave orders to one of the officers standing by to strike Jesus with his hand. (18:19-22) After the questioning, he sent Jesus "bound" to Caiaphas.

He was undoubtedly the ruling voice in the council that condemned Jesus, although nothing is said about his part in the proceedings that followed the preliminary questioning. He was present at the meeting of the Sanhedrin before which Peter and John defended themselves for preaching the Gospel of the Resurrection. (Acts 4:6)

He lived to an old age, and had five sons also appointed as high priests. (*The Antiquities of the Jews*, XVI 11. ii. 1, 2; XX. ix. 1)

## Bar Kochba

The Jews were outraged when Hadrian decided to transform Jerusalem into a city-state, modeled after the Greek *polis*. This action led to one of the single greatest revolts in the Roman era, led by Simon Bar Kochba in 132 A.D.

He organized a "guerilla" type army, which actually succeeded in throwing the Romans out of Jerusalem and establishing an independent Jewish State—although it lasted only a short time, about two and a half years.

His revolutionary success led many at the time, including Akiva, one of Israel's wisest and holiest Rabbis, to think Bar Kochba could be Israel's Messiah.

## Caiaphas

His name means "searcher." He was appointed high priest and continued in office from 19 to 37 A.D., when the proconsul Vitellius deposed him. He was the president of the Jewish council (Sanhedrin), which condemned the Lord Jesus to death, after Caiaphas declared Him to be guilty of blasphemy.

Caiaphas was the official high priest during the ministry and trial of Jesus (Matt 26:3, 57; Luke 3:2; John 11:49; 18:13, 14, 24, 28; Acts 4:6).

His successor was "Jonathan the son of Ananus," (Annas of the NT) (*Antiq.* XVIII. ii. 2; iv. 3).

The high priesthood of Caiaphas lasted some eighteen years. He was shrewd and adaptable enough to appease the Romans.

Neither Caiaphas nor his father-in-law is named in the gospel of Mark. He is first mentioned in the Gospel of Luke at the beginning of John the Baptist's ministry (Luke 3:1-3.) After Jesus had raised Lazarus from the dead, the Sanhedrin met to discuss what to do about Jesus and ultimately plotted Jesus' death. (John 11:47-54)

The Sanhedrin accepted the proposal of Caiaphas. John remarks that the words of Caiaphas were prophetic; they had a higher meaning than he realized. The suggestion to sacrifice Jesus to save the nation expressed the mystery of God's plan of salvation for all men through Christ's death.

As a Sadducee and opposed to the teaching of the resurrection, Caiaphas took a leading part in the persecution of the Early Church. The final appearance of Caiaphas by name in the New Testament is Acts 4:6. He is named second among the Sadducean leaders who assembled to try Peter and John. (Acts 4:5-12)

Caiaphas is no doubt that same high priest mentioned in Acts 5:17-21, 27; 7:1; 9:1 as the bitter persecutor of the Christians.

## CAESARS during the NEW TESTAMENT

### Augustus
Born at Rome on September 23, 63 B.C.
Died from an illness at Nola in Campania on August 19, 14 A.D. at age 77.
Reigned 41 years, from 27 B.C. to 14 A.D.

Augustus was the first Roman emperor, a grandnephew of Julius Caesar. He reigned at the time of the birth of Jesus Christ (Luke 2:1).

Arguably the greatest ruler of Rome, Caesar Augustus was a ruthless politician and soldier who used his power to restore order and prosperity to Rome with such success that his reign (27 B.C.-14 A.D.) became known as the Augustan Age. His birth name was Gaius Octavius, named as the adopted heir of his great uncle Julius Caesar in Caesar's will. At this point Octavius changed his name to Julius Caesar Octavianus; in his own era he was called Caesar, though in modern accounts he is usually called Octavian for clarity.

After the murder of Julius Caesar in 44 B.C., Octavian formed an uneasy alliance with Julius Caesar's fellow soldier Mark Antony and the general Marcus Lepidus, an alliance known as the Second Triumvirate. The three spent several years conquering their common enemies. It was at Philippi that Octavian and Antony confronted and defeated Brutus and Cassius (assassins of Julius Caesar) in 42 B.C. But Octavian and Antony finally turned on one another after Antony formed a political (and romantic) alliance with the Egyptian queen Cleopatra. Octavian defeated the combined forces of Antony and Cleopatra in the naval battle of Actium (31 B.C.) and became the absolute power in Rome.

In 27 B.C. the Roman Senate added to his adopted name of Caesar the title Augustus (meaning "divine" or "majestic"). As emperor he expanded the borders of Rome and took a particular interest in civic and cultural affairs, building temples and theaters, improving aqueducts and supporting poets and historians like Virgil and Ovid. Augustus died in 14 A.D. and was replaced by his stepson Tiberias, the son of Augustus's second wife, Livia.

The month of August (Latin *Augustus*) is named after Augustus; until his time it was called Sextilis (named so because it had been the sixth month of the original Roman calendar).

## Tiberius
Born at Rome on November 16, 42 B.C.
Died at Misenum on March 16, 37 A.D. at age 79 from being smothered with a pillow while on his deathbed with a terminal illness.
Reigned 23 years, from 14 to 37 A.D.

Tiberius was emperor at the time of the ministry and crucifixion of Jesus Christ (Luke 3:1).

## Caligula
Born at Antium (Anzio) on August 31, 12 A.D.
Died at Rome on January 24, 41 A.D. at age 19 from assassination.
Reigned 4 years, from 37 to 41 A.D.

## Claudius
Born at Lugdunum on August 1, 10 B.C.
Died at Rome on October 13, 54 A.D. at age 64 from eating deliberately poisoned mushrooms given to him by his wife Agrippina, Nero's mother.
Reigned 13 years, from 41 to 54 A.D.

## Nero
Born at Antium (Anzio) on December 15, 37 A.D.
Died at Rome on June 9, 68 A.D. at age 31 from suicide.
Reigned 14 years, from 54 to 68 A.D.

The Roman historian, Tacitus, wrote at length about Nero and the The Great Fire of Rome. I'll summarize the account.

The Great Fire of Rome erupted on the night of July 18 to July 19, 64 A.D. The fire started at the southeastern end of the Circus Maximus in shops selling flammable goods.

How large the fire was, is up for debate. It spread quickly and burned for five days. It completely destroyed four of fourteen Roman districts and severely damaged seven. The only other historian who lived through the period and mentioned the fire is Pliny the Elder who wrote about it in passing.

It is uncertain who or what actually caused the fire, whether accident or arson. Christians confessed to the crime, but it is not known whether these were false confessions induced by torture.

Later historians, Suetonius and Cassius Dio said that Nero sang the "Sack of Illium" in stage costume while the city burned. Tacitus' account has Nero in Antium at the time of the fire. He called the story of Nero playing his lyre and singing while the city burned only a rumor.

Upon hearing news of the fire, Nero rushed back to Rome to organize a relief effort, which he paid for from his own funds. After the fire, Nero opened his palaces to provide shelter for the homeless, and arranged for food supplies to be delivered in order to prevent starvation among the survivors. In the wake of the fire, he made a new urban development plan. Houses after the fire were spaced out, built in brick, and faced by porticos on wide roads. He also built a new palace complex in an area cleared by the fire. To find the necessary funds for the reconstruction, tributes were imposed on the provinces of the empire.

The populace searched for a scapegoat and rumors held Nero responsible. To diffuse blame, Nero targeted a sect called the Christians. He ordered Christians to be thrown to dogs, while others were crucified and burned.

Here are the words of Tacitus about it.

*"Consequently, to get rid of the report, Nero fastened the guilt and inflicted the most exquisite tortures on a class hated for their abominations, called Christians by the populace. Christus, from whom the name had its origin, suffered the extreme penalty during the reign*

*of Tiberius at the hands of one of our procurators, Pontius Pilatus, and a most mischievous superstition, thus checked for the moment, again broke out not only in Judea, the first source of the evil, but even in Rome, where all things hideous and shameful from every part of the world find their centre and become popular. Accordingly, an arrest was first made of all who pleaded guilty; then, upon their information, an immense multitude was convicted, not so much of the crime of firing the city, as of hatred against mankind. Mockery of every sort was added to their deaths. Covered with the skins of beasts, they were torn by dogs and perished, or were nailed to crosses, or were doomed to the flames and burnt, to serve as a nightly illumination, when daylight had expired."* (Tacitus: *Annals*, XV.44)

## Galba
Born near Tarracina on December 24, 3 B.C.
Died at Rome on January 15, 69 A.D. at age 72 from assassination.
Reigned 1 year, from 68 to 69 A.D.

## Otho
Born at Ferentium on April 28, 32 A.D.
Died at Brixellum on April 16, 69 A.D. at age 37 from suicide.
Reigned less than a year, during 69 A.D.

## Vitellius
Born on September 7, 12 A.D. (birthplace uncertain)
Died at Rome on December 20, 9 A.D. at age 57 from assassination.
Reigned less than a year, during 69 A.D.

## Vespasian
Born at Falacrinae on November 17, 9 A.D.
Died in Rome on June 23, 79 A.D. at age 70 of illness
Reigned 10 years, from 69 to 79 A.D.

Emperor during the Jewish revolt that led to the destruction of Jerusalem in 70 A.D.

**Titus**
  Born at Rome on December 30, 39 A.D.
  Died at Aquae Cutiliae on September 13, 81 A.D. at age 42 possibly of malaria.
  Reigned 2 years, from 79 to 81 A.D.

Before becoming emperor, he was the commander of the Roman forces that conquered Jerusalem and destroyed the Second Temple in 70 A.D.

**Domitian**
  Born at Rome on October 24, 51 A.D.
  Died at Rome on September 18, 96 A.D. at age 45 from assassination by someone in his household staff.
  Reigned 15 years, from 81 to 96 A.D.

During Domitian's reign John was exiled on the island of Patmos.

**Dead Sea Scrolls**

The Dead Sea Scrolls were documents written with a carbon based ink on both vellum (skins) and papyrus (paper). The first discovery was in 1947. Subsequent discoveries continued until 1956. Nearly 900 scrolls were discovered, over 200 which contained portions of the Hebrew Bible. They are the earliest extant manuscripts of the Bible, predating the Masoretic text by over a thousand years.

**Decapolis**: A league of ten Gentile cities in a large territory south of the Sea of Galilee and east of the Jordan River. They made an alliance for the purpose of trade and mutual protection from their enemies. Only one city of the Decapolis, Beth Shean, was west of the Jordan River.

**Essenes**

The Essenes emerged out of disgust with the Pharisees and Sadducees. This sect believed the others had corrupted the city and the Temple. They moved out of Jerusalem and lived a monastic life in the desert, adopting strict dietary laws and a commitment to celibacy. Many scholars believe that John the Baptist came for this group, or was heavily influenced by them.

The Essenes are particularly interesting to scholars because they are believed to be an offshoot of the group that lived in Qumran, near the Dead Sea. In 1947, a Bedouin shepherd stumbled into a cave containing various ancient artifacts and jars containing manuscripts describing the beliefs of the sect and events of the time.

The most important manuscripts, the Dead Sea Scrolls, were the earliest known copies of the Old Testament.

## Hasmoneans

The Hasmoneans led in the struggle against the taxes, political and religious oppression of the Seleucids, namely, at that time, Antiochus Epiphanies. The founder of the family, Mattathias, died in 166 B.C. In turn, his sons, Judas Maccabeus, Jonathan, and Simon led in the struggle. Under their leadership religious persecution ended, religious autonomy was restored, taxes were reduced, and political independence was achieved.

Later Hasmoneans expanded Judea's boundaries to their greatest extent in years. Because this expansion placed so many burdens on the shoulder of the people, several uprising sprung up between 90-84 B.C., which were instigated by the Pharisees. Jannaeus cruelly suppressed the rebellions. Jannaeus' widow, Queen Salome Alexandra, made peace with the Pharisees and brought them into the government. Her death was followed by a civil war that ended with the intervention of Rome and the conquest of Judea in 63 B.C. by Pompey. The last Hasmonean, Antigonus (40–37 B.C.), was deposed and executed by Herod the Great, who established his own dynasty under Roman protection.

# House of Herod

This House of Herod chart was created from material in the writings of Josephus, *Jewish Wars,* 1:562 and *Antiquities,* 17:191.

Herod the Great reigned as King of Judea from 40-4 B.C. Married ten times and with at least 15 children, I've charted only the most influential family members as they relate to the biblical narrative.

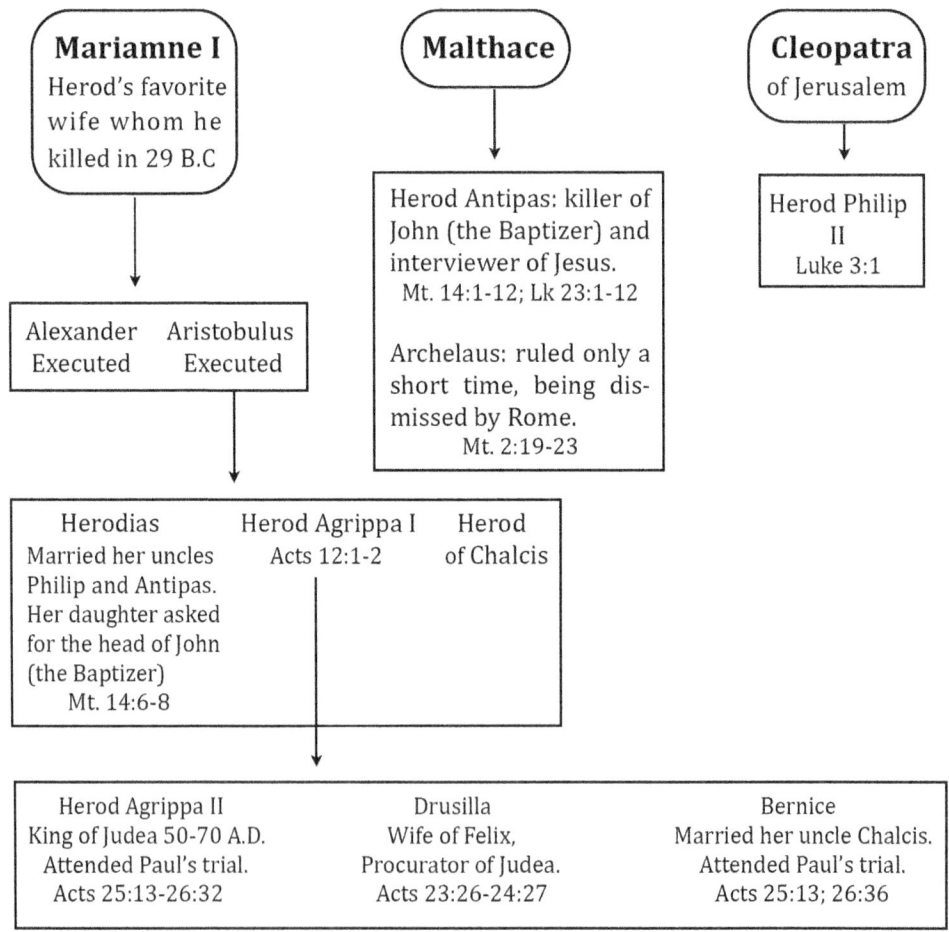

Someone has said that truth is stranger than fiction. That would certainly apply to the family that made up the Herodian Family—stranger than fiction! It was, at best, dysfunctional. Herod the Great brought many of his family members to mock trials and then had them executed. We know that he killed 2 brother-in-laws, his favorite wife and her grandfather, his mother-in-law, and at least 3 sons. This led Caesar Augustus, his old friend, Octavian, to say it was better to be Herod's pig than his son!

Who were the Herods? They are mentioned throughout the New Testament and not always very kindly. Even Jesus would say of Herod the Great's son, Antipas, *"Go and tell that fox, 'Behold, I cast out demons and perform cures today and tomorrow, and the third day I reach My goal.'"* (Luke 13:32 NASB)

Herod was the family name of several Roman rulers who served as provincial governors of Judea [as the Romans knew Palestine before 135 A.D.], and surrounding regions during New Testament times.

The first Herod, known as **Herod the Great**, was the Roman ruler of Judea during the days of Caesar Augustus when Jesus was born in Bethlehem (Mt. 2:1; Luke 3:1). All the other Herods mentioned in the New Testament were the sons or grandsons of this Herod.

Herod the Great ruled from 37–4 B.C., and was known as a master builder, organizer, and developer, although his policies were considered cruel and ruthless by the Jews. His most notable achievement was the rebuilding of the temple in Jerusalem, a project that took almost fifty years, long after his death.

He also rebuilt and enlarged the city of Caesarea into an impressive port city that rivaled Alexandria, Egypt. Josephus, the Jewish historian, said that it was built in such grand style that it was known as "Little Rome." Caesarea served as the Roman provincial capital for Judea during the New Testament era. Ruins of the magnificent aqueducts that he built at Caesarea are still visible today.

189

The historian, Josephus, describes the death of Herod at great length. I will summarize what happened:

Herod's health began to fail rapidly, so he was moved to his winter capital in Jericho. From there he was carried by stretcher to hot springs on the shores of the Dead Sea, but that did not help his condition so he returned home. Racked by despondency, he attempted suicide.

Rumors of the attempt caused loud wailing throughout the palace. Herod's son, imprisoned by his paranoid father, mistook the cries to mean his father was dead. Immediately, he tried to bribe his jailers, who reported the bribery attempt to Herod. The sick king ordered his son, Antipater, executed on the spot.

Now Herod plunged deeper into depression. He was only days away from his death. What seemed to bring him the most pain was the knowledge that his death would be met with joy in Judea. To forestall this, he devised an incredible plan. Here is how Josephus described it:

*"Having assembled the most distinguished men from every village from one end of Judea to the other, he ordered them to be locked in the hippodrome at Jericho."* Josephus, *Jewish Wars*

Herod then gave the order to execute them at the very moment he died. His sick mind reasoned that their death would dispel any joy in Judea over his own death. The order was never carried out.

After Herod's death, his body was carried in procession from Jericho to the Herodium outside Bethlehem for burial. Herod's body was adorned in purple, a crown of gold rested on his head, and a scepter of gold was placed in his hand. The bier bearing his body was made of gold and studded with jewels that sparkled as it was carried along under the desert sun. (See Herodion, pp. 83-84)

All of Herod's sons contested his will in Rome before Caesar Augustus. He decided to honor the will which divided Herod's kingdom into three territories. Three of his sons were given a part of his kingdom, but Augustus would not allow them to receive the title "King of Judea."

**Herod Antipas** was the son of Herod the Great. He was made the tetrarch (ruler of a quarter) of Galilee and Perea. Antipas' first task was to restore order caused by the rebellion of the Jewish Feast of Pentecost (Shavuot) in 4 B.C., which was a reaction to Herod the Great's death.

Antipas followed in his father's footsteps as a builder. He rebuilt Sepphoris in Galilee and Livia in Perea, but his most noted accomplishment was the construction of Tiberias as his capital on the western shore of the Sea of Galilee in 17 A.D. The city was named to honor his patron, Emperor Tiberias.

It was Herod Antipas that had John the Baptist executed. Antipas is best known for his role in the events surrounding the Passion of Jesus. Luke 23:6-12 records that Herod was in Jerusalem at the time. Upon inquiring Jesus' citizenship, Pilate was told that Jesus was a Galilean, thus under Herod's jurisdiction. Pilate sent Jesus to Herod. Initially, Herod acted pleased to see Jesus, asking to see him perform a miracle based on what he'd heard of him. But Jesus refused to do so and remained silent, even when questioned. After mocking and ridiculing Jesus, Herod sent him back to Pilate. This improved relations between Pilate and Herod, who had apparently been enemies previous to this occasion. Luke also records Jesus' trial before Herod, the only gospel to do so.

**Herod Archelaus** received the kingdom of Judea by the last will of his father, though a previous will had bequeathed it to his brother Antipas. He was proclaimed king by the army, but declined to assume the title until he had submitted his claims to Caesar Augustus in Rome. Before setting out, he quelled with the utmost cruelty a sedition of the Pharisees, slaying nearly three thousand of them. In Rome he was opposed by Antipas and by many of the Jews, who feared his cruelty. But in 4 B.C. Augustus, consenting to the will of Herod, allotted to him the greater part of the kingdom (Samaria, Judea, and Idumea) with the title of ethnarch.

According to Matthew's Gospel, Mary and Jesus fled to Egypt to avoid the Massacre of the Innocents. When Herod the Great died, Joseph was told by an angel in a dream to return to Israel (presumably to Bethlehem). However, upon hearing that Archelaus had succeeded his father as ruler of Judea he "was afraid", and was again notified in a dream to go to Galilee. This may be Matthew's explanation of why Jesus was born in Bethlehem in Judea but grew up in Nazareth. (Mt. 2:13-23)

**Herod Philip** or Philip the Tetrarch, was the son of Herod the Great and his fifth wife, Cleopatra of Jerusalem. He was the half-brother of Herod Antipas and Herod Archelaus. Philip inherited the northeast part of his father's kingdom and is mentioned briefly in the Bible by Luke. (3:1)

He married his niece Salome, the daughter of Herodias. She appears in the Bible in connection with the execution of John the Baptist.

Philip rebuilt the city of Caesarea Philippi, calling it by his own name to distinguish it from the Caesarea on the seacoast, which was the seat of the Roman government.

The maps on the next page show Herod's Kingdom and its division.

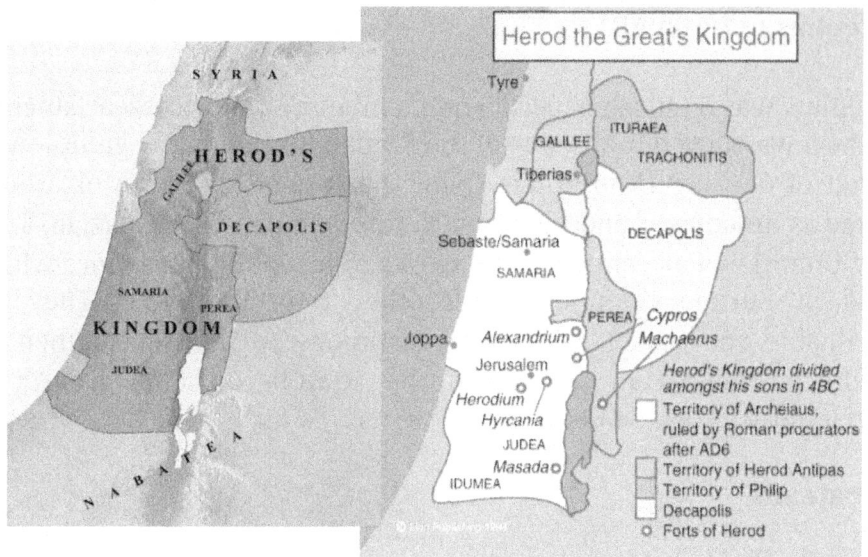

(Herod the Great's Kingdom Map: © 1994, Lion Publishing Co.)

**Herod Agrippa I** was the grandson of Herod the Great. In Acts 12, about the time of the Passover in 44 A.D., James, son of Zebedee and brother of John, was seized by Agrippa's order and put to death by beheading. Agrippa proceeded also to lay hands on Peter, and imprisoned him. But God sent an angel and released Peter from prison. After that Passover, Agrippa went to Caesarea, where the inhabitants of Tyre and Sidon waited on him to sue for peace.

According to Acts, Agrippa, gorgeously arrayed, received them in the stadium, and addressed them from a throne, while the audience cried out that his was "the voice of a god, not a man". But "the angel of the Lord smote him," and shortly afterwards he died, "eaten of worms." in 44 A.D. (Acts 12:20-23)

**Herod Agrippa II**, son of Agrippa I, was the seventh king, and last of the Herods.

In 53 A.D., he was made governor over the tetrarchy of Philip and Lysanias (Acts 25:13; 26:2, 7). It was before him and his sister Bernice that Paul pleaded his cause at Caesarea Maritima (Acts 26). He died at Rome in 100 A.D., thus ending the Herodian Dynasty.

## Josephus (37-100 AD)

Josephus was a Jewish general and member of the priestly aristocracy of the Jews, turned to the side of the Roman Empire in the great Jewish revolt of 66-70 A.D. Josephus spent the rest of his life in or around Rome as an advisor and historian to three emperors, Vespasian, Titus and Domitian. For centuries, the works of Josephus were more widely read in Europe than any book other than the Bible. They are invaluable sources of eyewitness testimony to the development of Western civilization, including the foundation and growth of Christianity in the 1st Century.

## Nabateans

Ancient Bedouin Arabs. These traders traveled in from Arabia and made their capital Petra, in modern day Jordan. They eventually controlled trade in perfumes and spices, and built numerous fortresses along the branch of the Spice Route in the Negev.

## Pharisee

The depiction of the Pharisees in the New Testament is not, for the most part, a positive one. Their name has even found its way into our English dictionaries associated with self-righteousness and hypocrisy. For example, the *Oxford English Dictionary* (subtitled, the definitive record of the English language) gives the following two definitions: "*n.* A person of the spirit or character commonly attributed to the Pharisees in the New Testament; a legalist or formalist; a self-righteous person, a hypocrite" and "*v.* to take credit to oneself for piety."

NOTE: There is a another definition pertaining to the Pharisees: "*n.* A member of a religious party within Judaism between the 2nd cent. B.C. and New Testament times, distinguished by its rigorous interpretation and observance of the written Mosaic Law as well as the traditions of the elders.

The Pharisees as a group probably started sometime in the 2nd century B.C., either before or during the Hasmonean revolt (about 150 years before the birth of Jesus).

The name 'Pharisee' comes from the Hebrew *perush/perushim* which means "to separate oneself" or "to explain" or "make clear". One might then say that the Pharisees were a group who were concerned primarily with the proper interpretation of the Bible and separated themselves from the things that God had told them to separate from—things which are in the Torah, the first 5 books of the Bible.

There are two major characteristics of the Pharisees, their meticulous observance of obligations under the Law for purity, tithing, and Sabbath observances; and their emphasis on oral law as equally binding to the Law.

The New Testament bears witnesses to their great concern over purity and tithing (see Mt. 23:23-26; Luke 11:39-42); and the many disputes Jesus had with them over the Sabbath day reflects it as well (see Mark 2:23, 27; Luke 14:1-6).

The other major characteristic of the Pharisees is the value they placed on oral traditions. "Oral law" refers to traditional rules and observances that were designed to adapt the written Law to the changes of time.

Josephus claims that this is the main issue between the Pharisees and the Sadducees. He writes that "the Pharisees delivered a great many observances by succession from their fathers, which are not written in the Law of Moses; the Sadducees reject them, and esteem only those observances to be obligatory that are in the written law" (Josephus, *Wars*, 2.162).

**Priest and High Priest**

In the New Testament, priests were a carry over from the Old Testament priests. There is nothing new or striking in the numerous references to their work. Perhaps the information of the greatest interest is found in Luke 1:5-9 to the effect that Zacharias was of the course of Abijah, the 8th of the 24 courses into which the priests were divided (see 1st Chron. 24:7-18), and that in these courses the priests divided their work by lot.

High Priests, as in ancient times, were the head of the priesthood. Until the time Isreal was taken over by foreign powers, High Priests were descendents of Levi, hence "Levitical Priesthood." As had been customary from Persian times, the high priest was nominated and/or appointed by the foreign power in control, regardless of lineage. The high priest in the time of Jesus' ministry was Joseph, surnamed Caiaphas, who held the office from 18 to 37 A.D. However, his father-in-law, Annas, who held the office from 6 to 15 A.D., still held a tremendous amount of power, as witnessed on the night Jesus was arrested. He was first taken to Annas (John 18:12-13).

## ORDER OF HIGH PRIESTS FROM HEROD THE GREAT TO THE DESTRUCTION OF JERUSALEM - 70 A.D.

Ananel, 37-36 B.C. (Appointed by Herod the Great)
Aristobulus III, 35 B.C.
Jesus, son of Phiabi, ? -22 B.C.
Simon, son of Boethus, 22-5 B.C.
Matthias, son of Theophilus, 5-4 B.C.
Joseph, son of Elam, 5 B.C.
Joezer, son of Boethus, 4 B.C.
Eleazar, son of Boethus, 4-1 B.C. - (Appointed by Herod Archelaus)
Jesus, son of Sie, 1 - 6 A.D.
Annas, 6-15 A.D. (Appointed by Quirinius)
Ishmael, son of Phiabi I, 15-16 A.D.
Eleazar, son of Annas, 16-17 A.D.
Simon, son of Kamithos, 17-18 A.D.

Joseph Caiaphas, 18-37 A.D.

Jonathan, son of Annas, 37 A.D.

Theophilus, son of Annas, 37-41 A.D.

Simon, son of Boethus, 41-43 A.D. (Appointed by Herod Agrippa I)

Matthias, son of Annas, 43-44 A.D.

Elionaius, son of Kantheras, 44-45 A.D.

Joseph, son of Kami, 45-47 A.D. (Appointed by Herod of Chalcis)

Ananias, son of Nebedaius, 47-55 A.D.

Ishmael, son of Phiabi III, 55-61 A.D. (Appointed by Herod Agrippa II)

Joseph Qabi, son of Simon, 61-62 A.D.

Ananus, son of Annas, 62 A.D.

Jesus, son of Damnaius, 62-65 A.D.

Joshua, son of Gamaliel, 63-65 A.D.

Matthias, son of Theophilus, 65-67 A.D.

Phinnias, son of Samuel, 67-70 A.D.

## Ptolemies:

The Ptolemies were the final dynasty of Egyptian pharaohs. Its founder, Ptolemy I Soter (323 B.C.), was Greek by birth. The empire began when Alexander the Great died without heirs, leaving his generals to divide all of Alexander's territory among themselves. The Ptolemies based the capital of their Egypt in Alexandria, a newly constructed port on the Mediterranean Sea. This dynasty ruled a powerful Hellenistic state that eventually stretched from Egypt to southern Syria. Arguably the most famous Ptolemy was Cleopatra, at whose death the dynasty ended in 30 B.C.

## Sadducee

One of the major difficulties in describing the Sadducees is that all that we know about them comes from their opponents. They themselves left no written record of their history, organization, or views. They appear on the scene about the time of the Hasmoneans, c. 200 B.C. and flourished until the fall of Jerusalem in 70 A.D.

A priestly and aristocratic group, the Sadducees owed their power to political alliance with the Romans, who ruled their land. They opposed the Pharisees' use of Oral Law and held only to the Pentateuch—the first five books of the Old Testament. They also differed with the Pharisees on many theological tenets: for example, they did not believe in resurrection and the immortality of the soul. (Mt. 22:23-33; Acts 4:1; 23:6-7) According to the New Testament, the Sadducees played a leading role in the trial and condemnation of Jesus (Annas and Caiaphas, according to the Josephus, were Sadducees. Interestingly, Annas had five sons, a son-in-law [Caiaphas], and a grandson who served as High Priests.)

## Scribe

The scribes make up another group of individuals who enjoyed the authority of leadership in Israel. In the New Testament they are associated with the Pharisees and the High Priests as opponents of Jesus. In the Mishnah they are presented as copyists and teachers. Josephus does not list them as a distinct group.

The scribes have a notable history. All ancient peoples had large numbers of scribes for the transmission of religious texts and other legal and historical documents. In the Old Testament the best known scribe is Ezra; because he was both a scribe and a priest, he was a very powerful religious leader. (see Ezra 7:6, 11)

# Additional Notes

## Additional Notes

# Additional Notes

## Additional Notes